PRAISE FOR ...

"*Speak Up, Dammit!* is a must-read, no matter where you are in your career! From tried-and-true communication techniques, to handling crucial conversations, to perspectives that will actively engage your every meeting, this book is the ultimate toolkit designed to help you share your voice."

—Marshall Goldsmith, New York Times #1 bestselling author of *Triggers, Mojo, and What Got You Here Won't Get You There*

"Finding and sharing our voice is one of the most important things we can do as leaders. This powerful book shows you how to step up and be heard!"

—Dorie Clark, author of *Stand Out* and executive education faculty, Duke University Fuqua School of Business

"The power of one's voice is crucial to success in any field. In *Speak Up, Dammit!*, Hope Timberlake provides the essential handbook for making your voice heard with clarity and confidence. Anyone can benefit from this book's practical advice, but women and individuals from underrepresented groups that often feel unheard will find it especially helpful in quelling internal fears while overcoming external biases embedded in organizational culture."

—Gloria Feldt, Cofounder and President of Take The Lead; author of *Intentioning: Sex, Power, Pandemics, and How Women Will Take the Lead for (Everyone's) Good*

"If you are looking to literally amplify your voice, stand out from the crowd, and get noticed, you must read *Speak Up, Dammit!*. This book by renowned expert and communication coach Hope Timberlake includes powerful try-at-home exercises that will grow your confidence and skills to become a savvy speaker."

—Nyna Caputi, Founder of The Expat Woman and Her Success Society, Speaker and Educator

"*Speak Up, Dammit!* is ideal for introverts. The self-paced format and the individual exercises make it possible for introspective people everywhere to quiet their inner critic and develop the skills to confidently and credibly vocalize their ideas to the world."

—Matthew Pollard, bestselling author of *The Introvert's Edge* series

"An important part of living with strength and swagger is having the ability to share your ideas with confidence. *Speak Up, Dammit!* guides you through the steps to take to make sure your voice is heard."

- Jane Wilson, author of *The Up to No Good Club: Defining Your Life With Strength & Swagger*

Speak Up, Dammit!

How to Quiet Your Fears, Polish Your Presence, and Share Your Voice

Hope Timberlake

Speak Up, Dammit!

If you would like to purchase bulk copies of *Speak Up, Dammit* please send your request to hope@hopetimeberlake.com.

Printed in the United States of America.

Book design: Clarity Designworks

ISBN paperback: 978-1-7377984-0-8
ISBN ebook: 978-1-7377984-1-5

Contents

Author's Note

The stories in this book are based on real clients. For narrative purposes, the stories contain composite characters and dialogue, and time compression.

Also important to note: this book is not perfect. You will find typos and other errors. Like speaking up, this book's mission is to help women and "onlys" make progress—not achieve perfection.

Please reach out to me at hope@hopetimberlake.com to share your thoughts, challenges, and successes. I look forward to hearing from you!

Introduction

You've worked hard. You've achieved academic success. You've landed decent jobs and are longing for a more impressive title with a salary to match. You follow the rules to a "t" and consistently go the extra mile. You're known as a team player and, in performance reviews, your ratings routinely "exceed expectations."

Congratulations! You're crushing it . . . on paper.

Perhaps this is because you know what's expected of you, and you're now in the zone. You feel comfortable—at least some of the time—because it's in these types of situations that you can "perform." But what about the times when the rules are unwritten, when the expectations are more than the bullet points in a job description? What happens when you know you should contribute during a meeting but feel too intimidated to speak up? Or when you muster up the courage to share your voice, only to have your ideas shot down?

This book is for you if you have a hard time speaking up when:

- You are the only one in the room who looks like you
- You know the stakes are high
- You want to impress people who intimidate you
- You are in an unfamiliar environment
- You are in a room with people more tenured than you
- You worry that your contributions will be stupid or not additive

These types of situations likely make your heart race, your stomach drop, your palms sweat or your head spin.

Believe me, I've been there.

::

My first career in hospital outreach programs was rewarding, fulfilling, and demanding. I loved the challenge of long days spent writing grants and overseeing programs that benefited the community, even when 10 pm meetings were the norm. However, the job became increasingly taxing with a colicky newborn at home—and was downright impossible when child number two arrived. It was too much, and I was struggling.

So, at 32, I changed careers.

I needed work that fit with my new parenting role. Luckily, a friend offered me a position at her boutique public relations firm. I was elated. A new experience, a fresh start, hourly pay at a higher rate, plus an opportunity to dress up and interact with other adults. I could work regular daytime hours and prove I was an asset in the business world. I was equal parts excited and nervous. I wanted so much to excel.

Within weeks of joining the firm, I was asked to join an all-day off-site meeting to strategize a cutting-edge advertising agency's positioning for the upcoming year.

My new boss, Sophia, was supportive of my growth and delighted to have me join the meeting. "Naturally," she counseled, "we will dress to impress." I was hardly rocking my postpartum physique and my closet was full of outfits appropriate for hospital work (read: not cool).

I pulled together the few items that might pass for almost-trendy and fell in line behind Sophia as she strutted into the sleek suite of a swanky new hotel. As we walked in, Sophia air kissed our client, Jessica, who set the tone for the day: "This is about brainstorming, getting creative, sharing all ideas. I want to hear from everyone. No idea is too small!"

The rally cry had been made.

I smiled at Jessica as I felt the terror rise up in my throat. What was I doing here? I had no experience with advertising agencies. This was a big deal, and I had a barely passable outfit and zero experience in the industry. The effects of imposter syndrome settled into my chest like a ton of bricks and yet being a fly on the wall was simply not an option. I needed to get in the game and play big.

We explored web strategies and social media techniques by scribbling ideas on a rainbow of sticky notes, placing them in designated corners of the room. There was just one problem.

I was petrified to speak up.

My job, my friendship with Sophia, and my self-worth depended on my contribution, but I felt like a deer in headlights. Despite Jessica's encouragement, I felt too mortified to contribute. I didn't have the confidence to stand up in my ill-fitting pants much less share a single thought. How could I possibly add value?

The more time that elapsed, the more pressure I felt to say something. The longer I stayed quiet, the more self-doubt I felt creeping in. I couldn't pay attention to any of the messaging, because I was knee-deep in this maddening cycle.

Jessica broke through my negative self-talk cyclone when she said, "We know social media is working wonders for the brown and fizzies." My opportunity had arrived. Remembering people appreciate questions, I asked, "Brown and fizzies?" The second the question escaped my lips, I felt free. At last! I spoke up, and felt my entire body relax as I let out a deep exhale.

Jessica replied dismissively, "The carbonated beverage sector." She was clearly annoyed that I had disrupted a brilliant brainstorm with a question so . . . elementary. The heat rose up my body, and my cheeks reddened. I was stunned into silence and wanted to die.

Finally, I had found the courage to ask a question, but the answer was obvious to everyone in the room. I couldn't wait for this day to end. And when it finally did, my inner critic marched on. I replayed the scene and my humiliation over and over. It felt like a nightmare.

Why Speak Up?

After what I now consider my "brown and fizzy" turning point, I began to share my voice in order to keep my new job that offered better hours and more money. Now, years later, I have the clarity to see I was not at risk of losing my job. Sophia had never expressed disappointment. But at the time I felt diminished, unworthy, and useless. I wanted to redeem myself, and was determined to prove my worth in the corporate world.

In your case, speaking up may be an opportunity to:

- Raise your visibility
- Build new skills
- Share your story
- Become a role model for others
- Show that a woman or person of color has an important perspective to share
- Feel confident, fulfilled, or validated

There are also cultural and organizational benefits to speaking up. The more diversity that exists among voices at work, the better the decisions, products, innovation, and creativity that get out into the world. Incorporating differing opinions also helps reduce risk and increase profitability.

In addition, speaking up reduces group think: the problem that arises when people agree with or don't challenge the majority opinion. Research shows that women are "likely to identify different things as problems" and "bring new perspectives and solutions."[1] Integrating differing viewpoints creates better decisions in business, in politics, and likely in every other field.

Obstacles to Speaking Up

Work Dynamics

Despite the compelling reasons to share our voice, many of us don't do it. Why? Perhaps it's due to work dynamics: the real or perceived differences in power which affect how we interact with others. We feel certain we'll get interrupted or that our voices will be drowned out. Or perhaps we fear we will be ignored or that we won't be provided an opportunity to speak up amidst the politicking and clamoring of other meeting attendees. Or maybe we simply don't want to take part in the

1 Rogers, Brittany K. "When Women Don't Speak." *BYU Magazine*, 2020.

game we see taking place, where others take credit for our ideas . . . even going so far as to use our own words.

These are not simply feelings or fears. The data support the experience of women facing conflicts, both overt and subtle. Women "are more likely to have their abilities challenged [and] to be subjected to unprofessional and demeaning remarks."[2]

Speaking up is particularly difficult when you are an "only." This term refers to a person on a team or in a meeting who is the only one of that race, gender, sexual orientation, communication style, etc. The odds of being an "only" increase if you are in a technical role, a senior position, or are a woman of color or LGBTQIA. Over 80% of women "onlys" are on the receiving end of microaggressions, including everyday sexism and racism.[3] As one woman shared, "I have to worry about how I'm perceived. I have to get comfortable with the risk."

It's no wonder we don't speak up.

We also don't share our ideas because we think it won't make a difference. We suspect our recommendations won't be implemented. But here's the thing. Do you *know* that speaking up won't make an impact? And what are the consequences of *not* speaking up? Not sharing your voice, when you have the ability to do so, implies your acceptance of the status quo, and you end up acquiescing to the look and feel of corporate leadership. And yet it's time for this kind of script—which one of my clients describes as "pale, male, and stale"—to get kicked to the curb.

When I transitioned from a man to a woman, I was asked if there was anything that surprised me about being a woman. My response, "I was never prepared to be discounted or disregarded. As a man, when I stated my opinion, it was rarely ever challenged or questioned. My experience and knowledge spoke for itself. As a woman,

2 Greenfield, Rebecca. "'The Onlys': There Still Aren't Enough Women at the Table." *BloombergQuint*, 23 Oct. 2018.

3 Coury, Sarah, et al. "Women in the Workplace 2020." *McKinsey & Company*, McKinsey & Company, 8 Oct. 2020.

I am often questioned and having to detail and explain my point of view. Once it is accepted by one of the men, it becomes so."

- A speaker in a gender sensitivity training

Self-doubt

Another reason we don't speak up is because we worry about our capabilities. We fear we don't have enough experience or that we haven't done enough preparation or research. Maybe the reason for our hesitation is because we question whether or not we have a fully fleshed out point of view.

Even today, years after my "brown and fizzy" moment, my self-doubt still rears its ugly head. As a communication coach, I have spoken to large crowds and led hundreds of corporate workshops. Each time, my nerves emerge. But after years of speaking, I know how to prepare my content and my mindset, to manage my nerves, and to create an experience that is fulfilling for both the audience and me.

Our resistance to speaking up? Well, it's universal. I have coached more than 2,000 male and female leaders in nearly every position. Here's what I've discovered: nobody knows all the rules. And, even at the tippy top of the corporate ladder, they do not feel comfortable nor in control when they are speaking in a new environment or to new people. This is simply a ubiquitous human condition.

You may be thinking, "Nope, not possible. My CEO looks calm, cool, and collected every time she speaks." That may be how she appears to you, and she may be truly comfortable speaking at an all-hands meeting because she has loads of experience under her belt. But is she as composed when she is in front of the board of directors? Or when she is pitching investors?

Here's the other truth: she may look like she's got her shit together but we don't know how she is truly feeling. We don't know what thoughts race through her head, if her palms are sweaty or if she fidgets under the table.

Let's face it, navigating work environments can be messy. We encounter many experiences where we don't know the rules and when we don't feel in control. While we cannot completely change nor control our environment, commit to learning, practicing, and repeating the methods in this book, and you will be able to overcome obstacles and feel comfortable speaking in new environments—even when the stakes feel high.

What If You Don't Want to Speak Up?

I am not here to push you out onto the stage. You, like most of us, likely have an aversion to being told what to do. Just look at the wide range of reactions to Facebook exec Sheryl Sandberg's *Lean In*.

What I am here to say is this: if you want to advance your career and have your voice heard, the development of these skills is crucial. I have worked with countless women who are often seen as the most experienced or the most knowledgeable person in the room. One would think they would be promoted based on their intellect and expertise. Unfortunately, time and time again, I've observed that being the best thinker in the room does *not* get you promoted—unless you share your ideas and communicate to others.

And just as important: both your organization and community will benefit when you speak up. Sure, you can write a blog to communicate your point of view, but profound change comes from verbalizing your perspective. This visibility is a direct path to the leadership suite, where corporate decisions are made. And let me assure you that expressing your ideas is as important to your personal health as it is to the health of your business and the world around you.

What Does Speaking Up Mean?

Speaking up means sharing your ideas and thoughts even when it feels uncomfortable. It is contributing when you are not sure how the listener will respond. It is participating in the discussion rather than spending time thinking, researching or perfecting your contribution.

My pledge within these pages is to provide you with the tools and exercises you need to develop the mindset, content, and skills to:

- Feel brave
- Take initiative
- Push through vulnerability
- Share relevant content
- Engage your listeners
- Speak in a compelling manner
- Look (and feel) confident
- Overcome obstacles to help you share your ideas at work

The Speak Up Exercises

Each chapter contains exercises that are thoroughly vetted and intentionally designed to help you build a specific communication "muscle." Some may not be easy for you to do at a specific time (for example, if you're on a plane or reading in bed at 11:30 pm). Or you may feel you're not ready to commit to that exercise because it sounds intimidating or weird or perhaps too elementary. You may find you want to jump ahead to the "advanced stuff" but know this: *the fundamentals matter*. I coach a broad range of clients—from babyfaced graduates to seasoned CEOs—using these exact methods. I highly encourage you to try each exercise—at least once—and, for some, you will want to practice them over and over. Trust me. The more time and energy you invest, the better results you will see.

In addition to the exercises, many of the chapters have questions for you to answer. To document your progress, it's helpful to dedicate a journal to capture your Q&As.

Remember, this book is not about turning you into a robot nor is it requiring you to follow every step. It's about creating the most authentic version of yourself. For those of you who set the bar high in every aspect of your life, you may feel nervous about doing everything "right."

But the good news is you can check your perfectionism at the door. While there is no wizardry in becoming a Speak Up maven, polishing two or three areas will significantly improve your communication game.

The important thing to remember is when you focus on the trifecta of courageous presence, compelling content, and smooth delivery, you will experience the magic of speaking up at work. And hopefully this will translate to your life, too. This process has worked for my thousands of coaching clients, it's worked for me, and it will work for you, too.

Why Speak Up?

Answering the following questions will help you clarify your communication goals:

- What is *your* definition of speaking up?
- What do you hope to gain by reading and completing this book?
- What could you create or change by sharing your voice?
- What might happen if you don't share your ideas?

Think about how speaking up will benefit your . . .

1. Relationship
    - With your company's leadership?
    - With colleagues?
2. Performance
    - In your role?
    - Your career?
    - Your reputation at work?
    - Your perception among those who are younger or newer in their career than you?
3. Personal Satisfaction
    - Your confidence?
    - Feelings of satisfaction?
    - Feelings of accomplishment?

CHAPTER 1
Pause

Gabriela is a proud data nerd who loves her role as an analyst at PetBest, an online pet supply company. She's responsible for customer surveys and, each month, compiles consumer opinions in order to improve online shopping experience.

Last spring, Gabriela arrived at the monthly meeting, prepared as usual. She had sliced and diced the data, formatting the results into beautiful pie charts and embellished tables that matched the company branding.

At the start of her presentation, Gabriela advanced to an overview of the consumer feedback and then said, "So, um, here are this month's customer survey results and, you know, the pie chart shows how satisfied the customers are with their, uh, overall website experience. And so the important thing to, ah, highlight is that 80% of, uh, shoppers rated the site's ease-of-use as like a four or five and this is, um, dramatically higher than, you know, the rating from three months ago."

When the meeting ended, Gabriela and her manager, Simone, met to debrief. Gabriela knew the information she shared was relevant and well received, so she was stunned when Simone wrote "improve gravitas" as a goal for Gabriela during her year-end review.

"Gravitas?" Gabriela thought to herself. "What does Simone mean by gravitas?" She asked her to elaborate.

"You identify and highlight accurate insights from the survey data. But during the monthly meetings you come across as, well, junior. I am not sure exactly why—it's just the impression I get when you present."

Gabriela was perplexed. She wanted to meet Simone's expectations, but had no idea how to be perceived as "more senior."

Simone offered to provide Gabriela with a communications coach, which is where I came into the story.

After Gabriela explained the situation to me, we made a two-part plan: first, Gabriela would deliver a mock presentation to me. Next, we would review video recordings of this as well as the recent presentation she had delivered to her team.

During this process, we discovered Gabriela's communication traits:

- She uses filler words (um, uh, like) and run-on sentences more than twice as often when she speaks with her team compared to when she speaks one-on-one with me.
- After the first two minutes of her presentations, Gabriela uses fewer filler words, but she continues to speak in run-on sentences.
- The only time she pauses is when she transitions slides.

The good news is Gabriela's communication foibles could be improved with adding one behavior: the pause. I explained that using a pause is key to replacing filler words and phrases. The pause also creates shorter, more impactful sentences, and an impression of confidence and control. It also conveys what Simone was seeking: gravitas.

After reviewing her presentations, we worked through how to add pauses to her communication and created an "exercise regimen" to establish Gabriela's new pausing habit.

The result of this work? The next time Gabriela spoke at a monthly meeting, she inserted more pauses into her presentation. The run-on sentences nearly disappeared, but she still used more filler words than desired. She continued to practice pausing exercises and, within weeks, she had dramatically reduced her filler words and improved her overall presentation style. Three months after Simone had given Gabriela her "gravitas" marching orders, she told Gabriela she noticed a difference in her communication. By the end of the year, Gabriela received her hard-earned promotion from Analyst to Specialist and was rewarded with a salary increase, an extra week of vacation, and more interaction with the leadership team.

::

Gabriela was told she needed to improve her overall poise, but she had never considered pausing as the solution to her problem. She is like many people who come to me for coaching: they show up with one problem whose solution is seemingly unrelated. This is similar to the patient who arrives at the chiropractor's office with hip pain, which is then resolved with an adjustment made to her neck. Our communication behaviors, like individual body pains, are part of a larger system. Often a tweak to one element of the system dispels the pain in another.

Two of the most common reasons people come to me for coaching:

1. They worry that they ramble or are not concise
2. The desire to feel and appear more confident

No one ever arrives saying, "I don't know how to pause" or "I need to develop eye contact." Once we review videos of their communication, we discover that 95% of the time,* their presentation delivery problems can be solved by three things:

1. Pause more often
2. Connect with listeners
3. Increase energy

The next three chapters cover the three physical delivery behaviors that will transform your communication style and greatly impact how you are perceived.

**You may be wondering about the solution for the other 5% of the time. Chapter 4 on Voice covers that.*

Pause

Although clients never come to me to work on this, pausing is the remedy for two of their top concerns: concision and confidence. Pauses are so impactful because they:

1. Capture your listeners' attention

When speakers share a long "essay" of information, they often sound flat, causing their listeners to tune out. A pause, or short silence, regains the audience's attention.

The televised Peanuts cartoons illustrate what happens when we don't captivate our audience. The characters in these holiday classics are kids, and when their parents or teachers speak, Charlie Brown and his friends hear, "wah, wah, wah, wamp, wah." It's a great reminder that when you speak in a monotone voice or continuously without a break, you risk losing the engagement of your listeners.

Christine Lagarde, President of the European Central Bank, communicates to large groups of people, mostly men, and often experiences them not paying attention when she speaks. She explains, "One of the things I have found most effective is to pause, because people suddenly think that maybe something is wrong, and they pay attention again."[4]

2. Reduce filler words and phrases

Adding "like," "so," "you know," "kinda," "um," and "ah," when you speak is a common habit—more than three-quarters of my 2,000 clients insert filler words into their communication. This habit appears most often when a speaker links sentences with a seemingly innocuous "and" or "so." This turns your distinct ideas into run-on paragraphs of information that even the most focused listener can't process.

The tendency to add "unnecessary words" stems from:

- Feeling obligated to fill the space
- Feeling uncomfortable with silence
- Buying time to think about what to say next

---

4 Hicks, Kathleen. "'The Economic Imperative of Empowering Women - A Conversation with Christine Lagarde.'" *Center for Strategic and International Studies*, 15 Oct. 2020.

The pause helps both you, the speaker, *and* your listener in the following ways:

You Use Filler Words because You:	Why a Pause Helps:
Feel obligated to fill the space	Your listeners appreciate a break and gain time to absorb your content
Feel uncomfortable with silence	The pause may feel long to you, but it does not feel long to your listeners
Need time to think	A pause provides time to think without the distracting noise of a filler word

3. Regulate your pace

Many speakers want to get "off stage" as quickly as possible and speak rapidly to "get it over with." Unfortunately, your audience cannot pay attention when you spew information. They become overwhelmed and your content becomes noise. Speaking too quickly, similar to speaking in a monotone, causes listeners to tune out because, once again, what they hear is the "wah, wah, wamp" noise that Charlie Brown and his friends hear from adults. The result? Disengagement.

Pausing also helps temper a speaker's pace. When people are told they speak too quickly (or they hear themselves speaking too quickly), they try to remedy the situation by s p e a k i n g v e r y s l o w l y. Yes, this literally slows down your pace, but it also makes you sound monotonous. Instead of slowing your pace to a tedious extent, maintain your energy, enunciate your words, and *pause* regularly to give your listeners time to hear and absorb your information.

4. Think and breathe

Pausing is beneficial not only for your audience but also for you as a speaker. It provides an opportunity to think and breathe. Research studies show we think between 400 and 4,000 words per minute.[5] If we

5 Beck, Julie. "The Running Conversation in Your Head." *The Atlantic*, 23 Nov. 2016.

pause instead of saying "um," we give ourselves the opportunity and space to decide what we want to say next.

The other benefit that a pause provides is an opportunity for you to take a breath. You don't want to feel breathless when speaking and your listeners don't want to be distracted by your short-winded communication.

5. Create the impression of confidence

When a speaker intentionally pauses during her communication, she appears confident. The unattributed adage, "confidence is quiet, insecurities are loud" underscores why pauses are perceived positively. As many of us can attest, sitting in silence requires—and exudes—confidence. When you speak, you may worry you need to fill the space or continue to explain your ideas. But by doing so, you are revealing your insecurities. When a speaker pauses and owns her silence, she is saying, "I own this space and I am saying something important." She conveys confidence.

Barbara Jordan, the first Southern Black woman elected to the United States Congress, is an example of a famous orator who confidently uses the pause to capture attention, regulate her pace, breathe, and avoid filler words. In 1992, she spoke at the Democratic National Convention, where she captivated the audience at Madison Square Garden. Barbara epitomized strength, control, and confidence through the delivery of her speech:

> "It was at this time. It was at this place. It was at this event. 16 years ago. I presented a keynote address to the Democratic National Convention. I remind you. With modesty. I remind you that that year. 1976. We won the presidency. We won it.
>
> Why not? Why not repeat that performance. In 1992? We can do it. We can do it. We can do it.
>
> What we need to do, Democrats. Is believe that it is possible to win. It. Is. Possible. We can. Do it."

Her words were measured and impactful, making her voice heard. Loud and clear.

> Sophie, a User Research Lead and often the youngest in her meetings, shared the following advice: "Be comfortable with silence. Do not feel like it's your responsibility to fill it. Especially if you have been asked a question, take a moment to think about it before you answer. I have seen many colleagues (mostly male) take a couple of seconds to mull over an answer, and it not only gives them time to order their thoughts, but it also gives gravity to their response and an impression that they've genuinely *thought* about it."

How Do You Pause?

Think of your speaking and pausing pattern as analogous to a butterfly swim stroke. To swim butterfly, a swimmer makes a big movement (the compelling content you share) followed by a glide (the pause.) In this way, the pause is less of an interruption and more an intentional vocal harmony.

To create pauses in your speech patterns, intentionally include them whenever you speak, and not just when you are searching for a word or about to utter a filler word. By adding pauses proactively (and not as a bail-out method), you are better able to rely on them when you need them. And you are establishing a calm presence, with confidence and control throughout. The exercises below provide more detail about how to pause.

How Long Do You Pause?

Pause for as long as it would take for you to say the words "you know." If you want to create drama before a big reveal, pause even longer. Your pause may feel long to you, but your listener is unlikely to notice. In other words, a pause is relative. A crude analogy is the pause feels as long to the speaker as the wait outside of a locked restroom feels to someone dying to "go." The good news is your listener—and the person inside the restroom—do not notice the time.

How Do Pauses Work in a Virtual Environment?

Due to the global impact of COVID-19, many of us had to make a pandemic pivot and, as a result, work from home, where we find ourselves meeting more commonly on screens. In a virtual environment, your listeners are more likely to multitask than they are in person. They are often sitting in a chair for hours on end distracted by open internet browsers, Slack, and the chiming of email. For these reasons, pauses are as—and possibly more—important when working virtually. After all, your listeners want to be engaged, they want to listen to a confident speaker, and are possibly annoyed by filler words that spill out when you don't take a pause.

> **"The right word may be effective, but no word was ever as effective as a rightly timed pause."**
>
> MARK TWAIN

EXERCISES

Exercise 1: Pause Assessment

What: Evaluate your pause effectiveness.

Why: How we perceive ourselves is different from how others see us. Listening to an audio of yourself will give you an accurate sense of how often you pause and where you could add more.

How:

1. Find a previously recorded presentation or conversation that you took part in. Or record audio of yourself following this prompt, "Describe your current role and your prior experience that led you here." Aim to speak for two or more minutes, and no less than 60 seconds.
2. Listen *without watching*. It may feel cringey and jarring because you don't hear yourself the same way in your head as you do when you play back the audio. For these reasons, it's good to listen a couple of times to get used to the sound of your voice before you are ready to listen for pauses.
3. Listen for:
   - Pauses (frequency and length)
   - Filler word and phrases (um, ah, uh, you know, like)
   - Linking words between sentences (so, and, and so)

Exercise 2: Investigative Research

What: Build awareness around your habits and your opportunities to pause.

Why: Observing and becoming aware of your behaviors is the best way to improve them.

How:

1. During low stakes conversations like dinner with friends, or casual conversations with colleagues and family members, begin to notice your patterns.

2. Specifically, pay attention to how often you:
   - Use filler words or phrases
   - Speak in run-on sentences or without a break
   - Continue to explain your ideas versus pause in between
   - Sit in silence when you have "the floor"

Exercise 3: Ball Toss

What: Use a ball to signify how long to pause.

Why: When we create a new habit (pausing) or replace an ineffective pattern (using filler words), it helps to utilize a physical movement to reinforce the new behavior.

How:
1. Find a small squishy ball, a tennis ball, or crumple a piece of paper into a ball.
2. Practice an update you might need to deliver at a meeting. After each statement, toss the ball from one hand to the other to represent a pause. For example, "Here's our plan to support district teachers." [toss ball] "First, we will ensure they are vaccinated before returning to the classroom." [toss ball] "Next, we'll provide a resource day for planning." [toss ball]
3. During meetings, you can keep your hands under the table or out of video range and toss the ball after uttering each statement.

CLIENT PERSPECTIVE

Ashley finds this exercise helpful in several ways. Tossing the ball helps her focus solely on the next statement to be communicated versus getting overwhelmed with the volume of content she needs to share. And because she is a fast talker, it moderates her pace. The ball toss also improves her posture because she needs to sit up to create space for the ball toss.

Another bonus? It keeps her hands busy since she can't fidget while presenting.

Exercise 4: "Veronica, I Give You"

What: The following series of three exercises requires you to move sticky notes that represent when to pause and for how long. In Exercise 4, you focus on pausing while speaking about everyday objects. Exercise 5 takes it a step further because you are asked to pause with the added pressure of thinking about work-related content. Exercise 6 raises the stakes even more by inserting pauses while you propose an idea to someone you look up to or want to impress.

Why: Practicing a new behavior while doing a physical activity (pulling sticky notes off a wall) increases the likelihood that it will become a habit.

How: Place five sticky notes on a wall at eye level two to three feet apart. Each sticky note represents one of your listeners. While looking at the first sticky note, say, "Veronica, I give you apples, bananas, and pineapple." The objects can be everyday things like a pen, paper, and notebook or more complex and fun like a trip to Paris, a walk along the Seine, and a moonlit dinner.

When you complete the phrase, remove the note from the wall and toss it on the ground. The time it takes to remove the note and toss it on the ground represents the amount of time you intentionally pause (or take a breath).

To see a demonstration of this exercise,
go to hopetimberlake.com/exercises

Important: Don't say a word while you remove the sticky note and toss it to the ground! This sounds easy but most people start the next "I give you" statement before they have paused.

Then move to the next sticky note and repeat, "Veronica, I give you . . . ." with three different objects. Continue until you have "given" items to all five sticky note "people" and paused between each "person."

Like many exercises in the book, this may feel silly, stupid, or too basic. This is normal. As voice and speech specialist and performance coach D'Arcy Webb (a.k.a. The Speech Diva) says about vocal training, "You have to accept the fact you're going to feel stupid when you're learning vocal exercises and be okay with making odd sounds." The same is true when you conduct exercises focused on eye contact, creating energy, and pauses. Trust that the process does indeed work! It has worked for my clients and it will work for you, too.

Exercise 5: "Veronica, My Role Involves . . ."

Why: This version provides an opportunity to practice pausing with content relevant to your job.

How: Repeat the "Veronica, I Give You" exercise with "real" content. This time you will describe your job to someone who does not know what you do. Explain your role in five or more digestible chunks punctuated by pauses. This is an exercise, *not a rehearsal*, which means your priority is to share small bites of information and speak in shorter sentences than you would ordinarily—and punctuate the short sentences with pauses.

The quality of the content you share is not important. In fact, to do this exercise you will need to simplify the complexity of your role.

For example:

- "I am a Project Coordinator at Yelp."
- "My role involves working with local businesses."
- "I make sure businesses in my territory engage with their Yelp profile."
- "Engagement includes keeping their profile current."

Record yourself sharing these snippets of information, punctuated by pauses. Listen to the recording and note the difference between how long the pauses felt versus how they sound.

Does your recording sound droning or unchanging? Do you feel robotic speaking this way? If you answered yes, don't worry, you are on the right track. It's awkward at first because our brains can only focus on one area at a time. Keep practicing and eventually it will flow smoothly, I promise!

Exercise 6: "Veronica, Here is My Important Idea"

Why: In this version, you practice pausing while sharing a recommendation.

How: Repeat the above "Veronica . . . " method using a recommendation you would like to share at a meeting or with your boss.

Here is an example:

- As a result of the company merger, we need to streamline processes.
- One way to do that is to meet with the Customer Success team.
- I'd like to contact the head of Customer Success to propose weekly meetings.
- Would you introduce me by email and I will take it from there?

Pro Tip: Listening to your recordings is hard. Our inner critic rears its ugly head every time we do something new, and we tend to focus on the things we don't like rather than the things we do. Chapter 10 will provide strategies for reframing critical thoughts. In the meantime, congratulate yourself for doing this work. You are making progress! Give yourself a pat on the back, exhale, stretch, grab a snack, or take a break before diving into the next exercises.

Exercise 7: Um-ectomy

What: An exercise that involves speaking freely with a partner who notifies you when you use filler words and phrases.

Why: To bring awareness to how often we use filler words and phrases when we can take the opportunity to pause.

How:

1. Find a partner, ideally someone who also wants to increase their pauses and/or remove filler words from their communication style. One person will serve as a Speaker and the other as an Observer.
2. Both partners stand up to increase the pressure on the Speaker.
3. The Observer gives the Speaker a topic that she needs to discuss with no preparation. Topics could include:
   - The best vacation you've taken
   - Where you would like to be in 10 years
   - An embarrassing experience
   - Your freshman year of college
   - Changes you would make to your job

   The Speaker starts talking as soon as she receives her topic even if she can't think of anything to say.
4. The Observer listens for filler words and phrases (um, ah, eh, like, so, you know, kinda, sorta) and for opportunities to pause.
5. When the Speaker utters a filler word, the Observer repeats it back to her in a loud voice—right as she is saying it.
6. When the Speaker could break up her thoughts into separate ideas, the Observer puts up her hand in a "Stop" gesture to indicate that she should pause.

7. Continue the exercise until the Speaker is able to talk for three continuous minutes without uttering a filler word or using a run-on sentence.

Exercise 8: Computer Support

What: Use an app or software program to determine how often you use filler words and phrases.

Why: Behavior change requires consistent attention and practice over time.

How:
1. Download LikeSo, Ummo, or a similar app that lets you practice speaking while analyzing which filler words and phrases you use.
2. Sign up for Otter or another transcription program that syncs with your Zoom account. At the end of your calls, read the transcripts to see how often you used filler words or phrases.

CHAPTER 2

Connect

When Keisha graduated from college with a degree in Management, she was over the moon. Who would have thought that the young girl who skipped past Bronx housing projects on her way to elementary school would be the first in her family to attend college? Now, twelve years later she was being recruited by big-name companies with exceptional benefits packages. The options made her giddy with excitement. Should she work for the popular retail chain whose clothes had always been out of her price range? Or the cutting-edge electronics company based in California? Or take the role as a store manager of a rapidly growing restaurant chain?

She accepted the manager position at Skewers, a restaurant chain that focused on creating flavorful food served on kabob skewers. The company was expanding exponentially (hello, potential upside), the perks were top-notch (monthly massages? Why, yes, I will) and it didn't hurt that she was addicted to the Thai Spice skewer.

When Keisha first met her team, she felt validated by her decision. She relished getting to know each team member and listening to their ideas. When she trained new employees, she communicated clearly and often. She put her all into this job because it meant so much to her and her family.

Keisha also knew that a manager of a fast casual restaurant faces a big challenge: turnover. The average employee tenure in her industry was four months. Continually recruiting and training new hires created an emotional and logistical burden on the store manager and the team. Keisha's philosophy was to continually inspire and support her employees, which she demonstrated daily whenever a team member's shift started or ended. During these transition times, Keisha paused to look them in the eye, smile, and thank them—even when the store was teeming with customers. Her team greatly appreciated the efforts.

There was also the challenge of the regional manager, Alex. Keisha could listen and motivate her employees until the cows came home but when Alex arrived, he would immediately spot an error and loudly reprimand the employee, often in front of customers.

Worse, he did this while staring at the counter, the food containers, the wall . . . anywhere but at the employees themselves. Keisha's warm demeanor was the polar opposite of Alex's gruff style.

To offset Alex's focus on process over people, Keisha doubled down on her connection with her employees. Thankfully, it worked; Keisha's team members stayed an average of six months—50% longer than the industry average.

::

Keisha's story illustrates the importance of connecting with your audience. We typically don't realize how important connection is until we don't have it. Think about a presenter who looks down at her notes throughout her speech. Or a manager who looks at a screen during your one-on-one. Or the doctor who enters notes into a laptop as you sit half-clothed in a cold exam room. Eye contact and facial expressions show you care about your listeners as much as—or more than—delivering the message.

So, how does one create connection?

Eye Contact

Mastering an aptitude for the nuances of eye contact pays off in spades.

1. Increase trust and credibility

Eye contact shows your listener you are trustworthy. For example, if you interview for a job and the hiring manager asks a question, looking up at the ceiling before responding could give the impression that your answer is not accurate or truthful.

This applies at home, too. If you ask your housemate, "Did you eat the last piece of chocolate cake?" and he looks away while saying, "No," would you believe him?

When someone asks an important question like "Is the project on budget?" (or "Who finished the Doritos?") providing an answer while maintaining eye contact will increase your credibility.

Looking away while answering a question is a common response when people are trying to think of an answer. Unfortunately, looking away gives your listener the impression that you don't know the information (which may be the case) or that you are making up or lying about the answer (which is hopefully not the case). This is important because our face is a better predictor of our trustworthiness than the content we share. So, the next time someone asks a question like, "Is the project on budget?" create trust and connection with them by maintaining eye contact as you answer.

Exercise 4 of this chapter helps train your brain to think on your feet while continuing to hold eye contact.

2. Gauge your listener's reactions

Looking at each listener allows you to assess their engagement and read their reactions. This is how you know if you need to adapt your content or presentation style to meet their needs.

This chart helps decipher what each reaction means and how you should adapt to your listener.

Your Listener . . .	This Means the Listener is . . .	To Adapt:
Nods head, smiles and/or leans in	In agreement or is an encouraging listener	Continue as is and move to the next listener to gauge their reaction
Holds eye contact with you	Paying attention, engaged	Continue as is and move to the next listener to gauge their reaction
Takes notes	Hopefully engaged but could be writing about something else or writing to stay focused	Confirm their engagement by asking a specific question to determine their understanding
Furrows brow or looks quizzically	Confused	Recap, explain your content in a different way, and/or ask a specific question to determine their understanding
Looks away or nods off	Bored	Amp up your presentation content and delivery style

3. Shift your focus

Focusing on your listeners reminds you that speaking effectively is not one-directional. Instead, your communication should feel like a conversation, not like a presentation.

Looking at your listeners also provides an opportunity to think—and get curious—about them. This creates more listener engagement *and* transfers your attention away from self-criticism to your audience. Many clients dramatically improve their presence and their feelings of confidence when they shift from self-analysis to thinking about their listeners. Not only do their listeners benefit, but the speaker does as well. It's hard to be curiously engaged and fearful at the same time.

As you sit down with your listeners, ask yourself questions that focus on them. This could include "I wonder how they will use this content?" "I wonder which piece of information will resonate the most?" "I'm curious what next steps they'll identify."

4. Get grounded

Many clients fear that their audience is judging them. This is a normal reaction. After all, when you speak to 10 people in a room, you observe 20 eyes looking at you. That's intense!

When you scan a room, you absorb a lot of information. Consciously or subconsciously, you notice what people are wearing, their body language, facial expressions, whether they are nodding or grimacing, and whether they are engaged or distracted.

If, instead, you hold eye contact with an individual, you reduce the amount of input you process. Focusing on a single point is a practice used in yoga to increase the yogi's concentration. During balancing poses, a student who looks around the room will often wobble and fall out of the pose, but when they hold eye contact with a single spot, they are centered and therefore more stable.

The same analogy holds true for speaking. When you hold eye contact with a single listener, you lock onto that person as if you are having a one-on-one conversation, which is a grounding experience. Speaking to one person reduces distractions and feels familiar. Think about how often we hold one-on-one conversations. For most of us, this is more comfortable than speaking to a larger group.

How Do You Hold Eye Contact?

You need to hold eye contact with each individual for longer than you think. Some of you were told that good eye contact involves scanning an audience and engaging with Every. Single. Eye. in the audience. While that might make sense ("I don't want someone to think I don't care about them"), it's hard for a listener to feel connected to you when you scan their face and move on.

Try scanning eyes the next time you are seated for a meal with three or more people. Share a simple update about your day while shifting your view from person to person. Did you feel a bond with each individual?

As awkward as it may feel to the speaker, it's important to hold eye contact for at least three seconds. Yes, that's one-one thousand, two-one thousand, three-one thousand. Most clients will say that feels too long, but if you ask the listeners who were on the receiving end of the three-second eye contact, they feel like the speaker was paying attention to them, not staring them down.

Speakers worry they will be perceived as staring. The reality is when you speak to more than one listener, you will rarely hold eye contact for long. You will naturally feel compelled to look around the room.

For one-on-one conversations, the situation is more tricky because it's just the two of you. In these situations, you still hold eye contact for three seconds but not for five or more seconds (that's when it starts to get creepy).

Instead, pivot between your listener, then to a piece of paper or notebook in front of you or, if you're meeting in person, to a screen displaying your visuals, then back to the person. If you take a break by looking out the window or to your listener's side, he may think you are focused on something he cannot see.

Facial Expressions

A second way to connect with your listeners is through your expressions. Research shows that listeners create first impressions in 10 milliseconds,[6] and facial expressions are one of the most important indicators.

Through the 43 muscles in the human face, you can create many impressions including:

6 Boutin, Chad. "Snap Judgments Decide a Face's Character, Psychologist Finds." *Princeton University*, 22 Aug. 2006.

- Warmth and approachability with eye crinkles and smiles or an upturned mouth
- Curiosity with widened eyes and raised eyebrows
- Confusion with narrowed eyes and a furrowed brow
- Displeasure with downturned eyebrows and a tight mouth (or lips)

What happens when you don't use facial expressions (or perhaps hit the Botox too hard)? You appear flat, dispassionate, insincere or—yes—bitchy, none of which helps you bond with your listeners.

How to Use Facial Expressions to Create Connection

1. Start with a smile. When your listeners see this, they (often unconsciously) smile in return. This exchange creates a bond between you and your listeners and gives you more confidence.
2. Match your expressions with your content. My clients are often concerned about getting their information exactly right and default to their "thinking face." During a company meeting, Samara shared the new upgraded company benefits in a neutral, clinical way. When you speak about something positive like company benefits, make sure your face matches your words. Similarly, if you are sharing worrisome information or expressing frustration or confusion, you certainly don't want to smile.
3. Match your expressions with your intention. Identify why you are speaking and make sure that intent is reflected on your face. My client Jessica had a missed opportunity when she shared a motivational message via Zoom, "Although we have never faced a challenge like this, I have the utmost confidence in your ability to succeed." Jessica's attention was focused on sharing her screen and her motivational message came out flat. By not expressing her confidence, she appeared insincere, which can have a worse outcome than if she had said nothing at all.

4. Learn what your face looks like when you are nervous, scared, disappointed, frustrated, or even thinking. Everyone I coach has a natural nervous, thinking or otherwise not happy expression that doesn't convey warmth. While no one should be penalized for this, displaying a detached—or negative—expression simply doesn't cultivate a feeling of connection.
5. Learn to neutralize negative or indifferent expressions with a smile or by "lightening" your face. To do this, focus on something pleasant like:
   - why you like your content
   - who will benefit from your information
   - the ridiculous cuteness of your cat

Then, the next time your boss's boss raises her hand to ask you a question, you can counteract your fear with a more approachable face.

Connecting in a Virtual Environment

The irony of communicating in a virtual environment is we need to expend more energy and yet we feel less fulfilled than if we were to meet face to face. In virtual settings, we don't have an opportunity to observe micro-behaviors and therefore can't catalogue full body approachability. Instead, we are hyper-focused on eye contact and facial expressions, which leaves us feeling exhausted.

Eye contact is tricky in a virtual environment because it's difficult to know where to look. In the camera? At the listeners? Classic media training dictates that people should look directly into the camera so that listeners feel a connection. While this is an effective strategy when you are not able to see your listeners, looking in the camera feels awkward—and is less fulfilling—when there are live people on a nearby screen. Pivoting between the camera and the screen is also not effective as this balancing act increases your cognitive load. The worst option is looking at a second screen which is analogous to turning away from your listeners as you consult the whiteboard or your notes. And it's the quickest way to lose connection.

Solutions

1. Place the video image of your listener(s) as close to your camera as possible. This allows you to either look at the camera and see your audience in your periphery or look at your listeners while the camera catches your face making it appear like you are looking into the camera.
2. Assuming your listeners' faces are close enough to the camera, try to focus on their expressions. It's difficult to gauge their reactions if you aren't looking at them!
3. Hide your self-view. This bears repeating: *Hide. Your. Own. Face.* When the pandemic forced us to switch from in-person to virtual meetings, suddenly we had to work in front of a mirror. And the results aren't pretty. Seeing your face is distracting and we are more critical of ourselves when we see our reflection.[7] Sure, you may want to sneak a peek to make sure you don't have spinach in your teeth but after that initial pre-meeting check, hide your image.

"We shall never know all the good that a simple smile can do."

MOTHER TERESA, a nun who dedicated her life to caring for destitute and dying people in Calcutta, India.

7 Ramachanran, Vignesh. "Stanford Researchers Identify Four Causes for 'Zoom Fatigue' and Their Simple Fixes." *Stanford News*, 23 Feb. 2021.

EXERCISES

Exercise 1: Connection Assessment

What: Evaluate your ability to connect

Why: How we feel is different from how others perceive us. Observing a video of yourself will give you an accurate sense of how well you connect with eye contact and facial expressions.

How:

1. Find a recorded presentation or conversation (like a recorded Zoom). If you don't have one, video record the next meeting or conversation such as a one-on-one conversation with your manager.

   Note: virtual meetings are the easiest ones to record.

2. Watch *with the sound off* and keep an eye out for the following:

- Did you smile?
- Did you grimace?
- Did you make direct eye contact?
- Did you look up to think?
- Did you look down?
- Did your head nod while listening?

Pro Tip: Before you watch the video recordings, think about someone you love and respect. Rather than being self-critical, watch your video with the same compassion you would offer to a friend. Remember: this is a marathon, not a sprint, and you are doing the hard work to elevate your communication game. I promise you, it will pay off.

Exercise 2: Seated Silence

What: An exercise focused on staying silent while looking into another person's eyes.

Why: Getting comfortable with stillness is important for both pausing and eye contact. Specifically, this exercise focuses on:

- Feeling comfortable with people's eyes or attention on you
- Training your mind to think about your audience rather than your discomfort

How:

1. Place two chairs facing each other. Sit across from your partner with your knees touching.
2. Set a timer for 60 seconds.
3. Hold eye contact with your partner without looking away and without speaking. You must consistently hold their gaze (but you are allowed to blink).
4. After one minute, note how that experience felt. Some people find the exercise uncomfortable or even humorous at first. If that's true for you, continue practicing.

   Note: if you don't have a partner for this exercise, you can conduct this exercise alone by holding eye contact with yourself in the mirror for 60 seconds.

Katrine, a *Speak Up, Dammit!* reader, was surprised by the deceptively simple instructions for this task. She found the exercise difficult but also a great way to practice "switching [her] focus away from discomfort."

Exercise 3: 5 Items

What: An exercise that requires you to think while holding eye contact.

Why: Maintaining eye contact while you are thinking allows you to appear engaged. This exercise serves two purposes:

1. To practice focusing on your listener when you feel pressure. The exercise simulates the experience of coming up with an answer during a high stakes meeting.
2. To identify the habits that emerge when you think under pressure.

How:

1. Stand facing a partner at one arm's-length distance apart.
2. Hold eye contact with your partner while s/he asks you to name five items within a category. Examples of categories include:

Food:
- Types of pasta noodles
- Non-green vegetables
- Names of cereal

Geography:
- Names of mountain ranges
- European capitals
- South American countries

Fashion:
- Brands of shoes (or, more specific, brands of sneakers)
- Brands of bags

Entertainment:
- Horror movies
- Celebrities

3. Once your partner has identified a category for you, name five items within that category. You may not say anything else; no filler words (um, er, ah), no explanations ("I don't

really know pasta noodles because we don't eat pasta much"), no questions ("I know I said squash and corn. Did I also say red peppers?")

4. During the exercise, note whether you:

- Crowd the space with filler words or explanations
- Break eye contact while thinking
- Fidget

Once you know your tendencies, you can develop the skills to maintain calm and appear confident when you think under pressure.

5. Some categories are easier than others. With that in mind, repeat the exercise multiple times. Practice this exercise until you can answer consistently while maintaining a connection.

Pro tip: Looking into someone's eyes can feel intense. If you struggle with maintaining eye contact, give yourself a break by looking at your partner's eyebrows or at the bridge of her nose. While the ultimate goal is to maintain true eye contact, you can look at the "racoon mask" of her face, which can create the feeling of connection.

To see this exercise demonstrated, go to hopetimberlake.com/exercises

Exercise 4: "Veronica, I Give You" Repeat

What: Repeat the solo sticky note series used to practice pausing in Chapter 1. This time the focus is on eye contact.

Why: People have a hard time gauging how long to hold eye contact. While best practice dictates a speaker should do this for three to five seconds, no one can count to five while also thinking about their content (or at least they can't do both well).

In this exercise you hold "eye contact" with a sticky note for 3-5 seconds, represented by a solid one one-thousand, two one-thousand, three one-thousand (four one-thousand, five one-thousand). This is the right amount of time to build a connection with your listener, yet not so long that your eye contact feels creepy.

How:

1. Place five sticky notes on a wall at eye level two to three feet apart. Each sticky note will play the role of a listener.
2. Look at one sticky note at a time as if you are looking at a person who is attending your meeting. While maintaining "eye contact" with the sticky note, name three random items to give to Veronica, i.e., "Veronica, I give you apples, bananas, and pineapple."
3. When you complete the phrase, remove the sticky note from the wall and toss it on the ground. This action represents the pause from Chapter 1.
4. Move to the next sticky note and maintain "eye contact" while speaking to it. Repeat with each sticky note until you have "given" items to all five "people."
5. Pay attention to when you look up, down, or to the side to think.

Exercise 5: "Veronica, My Role Involves . . . "

Why: This version provides an opportunity to practice holding *eye contact* with content relevant to your job.

How:

1. Repeat the "Veronica, I Give You" exercise with "real" content. This time you will describe your job to someone who does not know what you do. Explain your role in five or more digestible bites.
2. During each piece of information, consistently hold eye contact with one sticky note. When you complete the phrase, remove the sticky note from the wall and toss it on the ground.

   For example, your digestible bites may sound like:

   - "I am a research scientist at XYZ Analytics."
   - "I analyze data collected by people's engagement on websites."
   - "I use the data to determine consumer trends."
   - "We sell our findings to companies that sell consumer products."
   - "The companies use the data to make decisions about where to advertise."
3. Pay attention to when you look away to think.

Note: This is an exercise, not a rehearsal. The goal is *not* to create compelling content. Let's be real. If you try to hold eye contact for three seconds *and* come up with engaging material, you will do neither well! Instead, focus on holding eye contact and sharing three seconds of *simple* content the first 5-10 times you do this practice. Once you have that down, repeat this exercise while increasing the complexity of your content.

Exercise 6: "Veronica, Here is My Important Idea"

Why: In this version, share a recommendation while holding *eye contact* with your listener.

How: Repeat the above "Veronica . . . " method while rehearsing a recommendation that you would share at a meeting or with your boss.

Reminder: hopetimberlake.com/exercises contains videos showing how this exercise looks

Exercise 7: Crumbled Ball Group Exercise

What: A partner or group exercise to practice holding eye contact for three to five seconds.

Why: Practicing a new behavior while doing something physiological helps build the skill.

How:

1. Gather a partner or, even better, a group of three or more people. You will also need a tennis ball, a squishy ball, or a sheet of paper you crumple into a ball. The ball represents the "ball" of information you want to share with your listeners.
2. Standing in a circle, hold eye contact with one listener while you throw the "ball" of information to that person. Continue to hold eye contact with the listener as they catch the ball and throw it back to you. This is a metaphor, obviously, as your listener throws back her response to the information you shared.
3. Once you catch her "response," hold eye contact with a second listener and toss the ball of information to them. Hold eye contact while they catch the ball and throw back their "response."
4. Repeat until every listener has caught several "balls of information."

Exercise 8: Everyday Practice

What: Everyday practice to reinforce the behavior of connecting.

Why: Holding eye contact without the aid of a sticky note or ball is hard to do. To create the new behavior, you need to prioritize practicing the skill.

How:
1. Practice holding eye contact during low-stakes situations like at dinner with family or friends.
2. Hold eye contact for the amount of time it would take to say, "Veronica, I give you a trip to Maui, a swimsuit, and a pina colada." It helps to envision your listener with a sticky note on her forehead that you look at for three seconds before moving to your next listener.

Exercise 9: Facial Expressions Exercise

What: Evaluate your facial expressions during work situations.

Why: We often do not have an objective way to determine how we are being perceived.

How:
1. Review recordings of your meetings with the sound off.
2. As you watch, what do you notice? Can you tell the difference between when you are thinking, interested, bored, annoyed, or excited? Which expressions would you change, if any?

CHAPTER 3
Energy

Stella faced a challenge. Her client, a high-end handbag company named Milo, requested new website functions to learn more about their shoppers. Stella's job was to make sure her client's website goals were met. Unfortunately, the engineers on Stella's team could not meet Milo's needs and she needed to deliver the bad news.

Stella knew if she disappointed her clients, she might risk losing the account and potentially her job. She asked to meet with the engineering team to brainstorm some alternatives. Although they could not determine the length of time shoppers spent browsing each item as the client wished, the engineers could create a survey gaming tool that assessed customers' style preferences.

Because she could not meet Milo's expectation, Stella was concerned how her client would respond to the gaming tool—yet her hands were tied. She spent countless hours creating slides that explained why the engineers could not track the time consumers spent browsing each item. She felt a lump in her throat every time she thought about how disappointed they would be.

As she fine-tuned her presentation, *30 Rock*, the sitcom, played in the background. On the show, Congresswoman Bookman, played by Queen Latifah, meets with the NBC brass to demand more diversity in their programming. Stella looked up from her presentation and saw Congresswoman Bookman sharing her opinion in a passionate, energized voice. She proclaimed, "The future! And America! Now I may have lost my train of thought several minutes ago, but if I continue to talk like this, no one will notice. And when I stop, you will applaud my energy! Thank you!"

"That's it," Stella thought. "Rather than apologizing for what we can't do, I can enthusiastically share the gaming tool to demonstrate what we can do."

Stella spent the rest of the evening focusing on how the gaming tool would meet Milo's demand to learn more about their customers. She highlighted the benefits of this solution and considered how she would excitedly present this alternative. As she rehearsed, she paid close attention to her voice, specifically her volume and emphasis, and also on smiling as she discussed the benefits of the gaming tool. The more she rehearsed her passionate delivery, the stronger her conviction grew that this was the right solution for Milo.

The next day, Stella entered the room and felt excited. She knew the gaming tool was good and, to make sure she demonstrated her passion, she channeled Queen Latifah's Congresswoman Bookman character.

She opened the meeting with, "As you know, we scheduled today's meeting to discuss the functions you requested last month. Before we discuss those details, I'd like to introduce you to some mock-ups of a gaming tool that will both inform us about Milo's shoppers and further engage them on the site. With that, let me present the Milo Style Gaming Tool!"

She showed different elements of how the tool would look and how it would operate. Milo's head of analytics looked intently, glanced at her team members and said, "Wow, I thought I wanted to know how long shoppers spend perusing each bag, but learning their style preferences will benefit both marketing and product design."

"Even better, this will increase customer engagement," Milo's chief marketer chimed in.

The head of revenue was last to speak. "This is really cool. I love it! Let's move forward."

With that, Stella subtly exhaled and said, "Great. I will make sure the engineers start on this right away. Now let's discuss the specific type of products you'd like to see included in the gaming tool."

That night, as Stella shared her day with her roommate over a glass of wine, she shook her head in disbelief. "I am shocked how well that went. I really thought I might lose the client—and my job! It's crazy that I spent so much time planning how to apologize to them when all they really needed was a solid idea, shared with enthusiasm."

Not only did Stella meet Milo's needs, they also increased their budget. They loved the gaming tool and Stella's support of their success. Stella's nudge to go big delivered her personal job security, and also positively impacted her company's bottom line. By enthusiastically supporting the alternative plan, she met Milo's immediate need. She also learned that presenting with passion creates more buy-in from stakeholders and elevates her visibility, important steps for expanding her role and her career.

::

There's no doubt about it, an impassioned delivery is crucial to articulating your message. Congresswoman Bookman, Jerry McGuire when he proclaims his manifesto, and Oprah Winfrey when she gives away new cars, all share one mighty component. They each exemplify passion by using their voice. They use their energy to motivate people and, in some cases (like Jerry Maguire), they get their listeners to consider ideas one might normally think are crazy.

Over 75% of my clients are more concerned with the content than they are with their physical delivery. The irony is all of them could better capture their listeners' attention simply by increasing their energy. And, in my experience of watching tens of thousands of videos, an animated delivery is more captivating and creates a longer, more positive impression than an accurate, detail-laden presentation.

So how do you create passion?

It's simple. Start by modulating your voice.

Passion through Modulation

Take a quick moment to revisit in your mind the educational streets of your youth. Reflect back on your school teachers and college professors, and the ways in which you would learn from them. Do you remember a favorite teacher whose lectures were more interesting because of their passion? You may have also experienced attending a mandatory college course that sounded downright boring on paper until you found the professor's engaging and quirky style to be infectious. Shockingly, you discovered the "magic" of statistics!

Now, contrast that experience with a course that aligned with your interests. You couldn't wait to take Social Media & Politics. The class was taught by Professor Simon, a pleasant looking thirtysomething man wearing a bow tie. Although the bow tie was surprising, more surprising was Professor Simon's voice. His quiet monotone put his students to sleep (nothing to do with your late-night college shenanigans, of course). Had his voice and style represented the interest that students felt when signing up for the course, they would have enjoyed the lectures and learned *so* much more.

And then there is the one-two punch of a boring topic taught by an equally dull teacher. Remember the economics teacher in Ferris Bueller? Although the teacher, played by Ben Stein, is most known for his droning lines of "Bueller? Bueller?" he also delivered a less-than-scintillating economics history lesson. "In 1930," he said, "the Republican-controlled House of Representatives, in an effort to alleviate the effects of the . . . Anyone? Anyone? . . . the Great Depression, passed the . . . Anyone? Anyone? The tariff bill? The Hawley-Smoot Tariff Act? Which . . . Anyone? Raised or lowered? . . . Raised tariffs."

Snore.

Had Ben Stein channeled his Comedy Central game show voice and given this same economics lesson with greater modulation, intentional pauses, and no "anyones", he would have captured *at least some* of the class's attention.

Rather than a monotone lecture, it could have sounded like: "In **1930**, the Republican-controlled House-of-Representatives, in an effort to ALLEVIATE the effects of [pause] the **GREAT. DEPRESSION**, passed a tariff bill [pause] **the Hawley-Smoot Tariff Act**, which [pause] **RAISED** tariffs." By adding modulation, pauses and varying his pace, even a topic as boring as tariffs can be fun and engaging.

Why Passion?

First, unlike teachers, whose primary role is to inform, your goal is to inspire. You want your listeners to feel something even when you're "just" sharing an update or reassuring your audience that the project is on track. Modulation is more important when your goal is to get your audience to take action.

Inspiring your listeners requires tapping into their emotional side with a passionate delivery. In workshops, we sometimes use the expression, "If you don't show it, they won't know it." (Hint: Exercise 2 will help you practice this.)

Next, our brains are hardwired for change,[8] which means you will lose your listeners' attention unless you vary your voice, emphasize specific words, raise and lower your tone, and diversify your volume.

Remember: Ben Stein in Ferris Bueller uses very little modulation. But Brené Brown, the influential Texan author and researcher, uses a lot, y'all!

Another reason to inject enthusiasm is that when you speak in an energetic tone, your listener is less likely to hear your filler words. This is not an excuse to use more; it is a strong motivator to deliver your words with passion.

Demonstrate Passion . . . on a Screen

A passionate delivery is even more important in virtual environments where a listener's sight is limited to a screen—and sometimes only to

8 Blatchford, Emily. "How Neuroplasticity Can Help You Get Rid Of Your Bad Habits." *HuffPost Australia.*, 21 Nov. 2017.

audio. Since speakers tend to sound less energetic while seated, consider standing up when you communicate in virtual and in-person environments.

Another tip? Double the amount of energy you think you need to exert. Your listeners are likely multitasking and distracted. When you double your energy, you are much more likely to capture their attention.

To do this, imagine there are twice as many participants in the meeting. For example, if you are presenting to a team of five people, imagine you need to capture the attention of a crowd of ten. If you are presenting to two people, exert the energy needed to present to a group of four.

You may be wondering how much energy is enough to capture the attention of four people. The truth is, we are not the best judge of our own performance. We may feel we are sharing information energetically and yet, once we listen or receive feedback, we find out our delivery was flat.

Conversely, we may have no idea that we inject too much enthusiasm into our speech patterns until we listen and realize we sound like an overly enthusiastic cheerleader.

Don't worry. Exercise 1 will help you assess your energy.

How Do You Increase Energy?

To create a passionate voice, vocal modulation is key. It's the energy we project through our voice by changing our pitch or tone. Put simply, modulation is what creates interest; it's how storytellers resonate and how adults express dialogue from children's books.

To improve your passion:

1. Emphasize specific words and phrases, and vary your pace and volume.
2. Identify an aspect of your content that interests you or your listeners. I know, presenting about risk avoidance strategies may not feel inherently exciting but every topic contains a benefit or impact that could be highlighted and communicated in an enthusiastic way.

3. Add large, purposeful gestures to illustrate your points.
4. Smile and use a variety of expressions.
5. Determine your range by reading a children's book, then apply that range to your work topics.

Exercises 2 and 3 focus on increasing modulation.

How Much Energy?

You may feel like you're overdoing it. If you are a sensitive person, highly attuned to small changes, increasing your energy even a single decibel will feel like a lot. Rather than trusting how it feels—particularly because all new things feel uncomfortable—record yourself and observe. What feels like overdoing it is likely "just right."

EXERCISES

Exercise 1: Energy Assessment

What: Evaluate your energy effectiveness

Why: How we feel while speaking is different from how others perceive us. Listening to an audio clip of yourself will give you an accurate sense of how passionate you sound and where you could add energy.

How:
1. Find a recorded presentation or conversation.
2. Listen to the recording, no matter how hard that is for you.
3. Listen for:
   - Modulation or variation in your voice
   - Alternating volume or pace
4. Watch for:
   - Gestures
   - Shifting expressions

Exercise 2: Passionate About a Paperclip

What: An exercise to improve inflection and volume.

Why: *How* you say it is often more important than *what* you are saying.

How:

1. Think of an activity, an experience, a vacation spot, or somebody you feel passionately about. It could be water-skiing, painting, traveling to remote locations, or your dog. Any topic of interest will work.
2. Video record yourself describing your passion in a flat, monotone manner. The words you share indicate your passion, but the style in which you present (your volume and inflection) suggests otherwise.
3. Next, look around the room and find an ordinary, inanimate object. This could be your computer charger or the light switch or the industrial carpet beneath your desk.
4. Video record yourself describing this object in the most passionate manner possible. Describe this item as if it is the most interesting item you have encountered all year.
5. Replay both recordings. What did you notice?

   Specifically compare your:
   - Voice when you described your passion versus when you described the inanimate object
   - Facial expressions
   - Gestures

It may feel ridiculous to share your passion in a boring way or to excitedly describe an inanimate object, but the point of this exercise is to see that even mundane topics (like light switches) can become interesting when you speak about them with enthusiasm.

Exercise 3: Entertain a Preschooler

What: Read a children's book

Why: Find your vocal and energetic range

How:
1. Find a children's book from the library, a neighbor, or online.
2. Read the book as if you were reading to a room of preschool children.
3. Record yourself while you read.
4. Play the recording back to hear your vocal range, volume changes, and emphasis.
5. Notice:
   - Where your vocal range was effective
   - When you felt you were speaking in an overly dramatic manner but the playback felt just right
   - Where you could amp up your energy even more

Exercise 4: Celebrity Announcer

What: Practice speaking in an energetic style

Why: Pro athletes "hyper-rehearse" to prepare themselves to excel during their games. For example, NBA basketball player Steph Curry practices throwing free-throw shots from the other end of the basketball court. By practicing from 90 feet away, when he needs to throw a 15-foot free throw, the challenge feels easy.

The same applies to speaking energetically. If you practice speaking in an overly enthusiastic way, your slightly tempered workplace version will meet your audience's needs.

How:
1. Think of your favorite celebrity. This could be a rockstar, athlete, writer, whomever.

2. Imagine introducing them to a stadium full of people. For example, if you choose Meghan Markle, you might say, "Ladies and gentlemen! I am honored to introduce to you MEGHAN - MARKLE! Please join me in giving MEGHAN MARKLE a rousing round of applause!"
3. Introduce your celebrity with the degree of enthusiasm this performer deserves.
4. Audio record your introduction.
5. Replay your introduction specifically asking yourself:
   - Did you deliver the introduction with the level of enthusiasm this person deserved?
   - If not, how can you increase your enthusiasm to introduce this performer in a way she or he deserves?
   - Can you identify an opportunity at work where you can bring this level of enthusiasm?

CHAPTER 4

Voice

Carmela was in a real conundrum. As interim President of Luxe, the scandal-ridden hotel chain, she had a career-defining challenge on her hands. First, Luxe was in crisis. After key members of the leadership were exposed for fueling a long-term hostile environment for women, the company's reputation was in the gutter. Even though the poorly behaving Luxe leaders had been forced out of the company, travelers continued to boycott the hotel chain. Revenue plummeted and the company was forced to lay off one-third of their employees. In order to retain the rest of the staff—and help rebuild the company—Carmela needed to ease the employees' concerns that they might be next on the chopping block.

Despite the dramatic scenario, Carmela was motivated by the recent changes. Removing the toxic leaders made it possible for Luxe to redefine itself as a socially conscious company. Unfortunately, the chain's revenue decline meant conscientious employees were also let go. Carmela wanted to share her excitement with the team, but also knew she needed to be sensitive to those discouraged about the dismissal of their colleagues.

Overshadowing these points was that as interim President, she had rarely presented to the company and few staff members were familiar with her. She wanted to transition into a permanent leadership role, but she needed to increase her visibility and prove herself to be worthy of captaining the ship.

The company's town hall meetings were the natural forum for Carmela to address and reassure her employees, to express her empathy for the loss of colleagues, to share her excitement about the company's potential, and—most importantly—to prove her credibility.

During the first town hall following the shake-up at Luxe, Carmela began with a note of compassion. She spoke in a soft voice at a deliberate pace while acknowledging how difficult the prior six months had been. Rather than sugarcoat the experience, she called out specific examples of tough moments that included the Wall Street Journal article that broke the story, the boycotting of the company, and the recent layoffs. She spoke in a stage-whisper, projecting loud enough for the room to hear but in a quiet tone that reflected an understanding of how difficult these situations had been for employees.

Next, she thanked the team members for sticking with Luxe. With a smile on her face that warmed her tone, Carmela spoke more loudly and increased her pace slightly which brought gratitude to her voice and words. She paused to allow the sincerity to sink in.

Then, she switched gears by saying, "And here is the good news. *We - have - a - plan*," emphasizing each word. "I've served at two other competitive hotel chains prior to my position as the head of strategy at Luxe. I know how to turn business around." Carmela spoke clearly, emphatically, and ended each sentence in a lower tone that indicated her assertive intent. "Would you like to hear my plan?" she asked in a faster-paced and lighter, higher tone. "Here - It - Is!" Carmela announced. With that, she illuminated a slide deck that showcased the main components of her plan. She spoke more quickly using greater emphasis and a wider vocal range. Carmela watched as employees leaned in closer with rapt attention.

By the end of her first town hall, it was clear Carmela had met her objectives. Employees felt heard. They were reassured and excited about the future. Four months later, Carmela was appointed as Luxe's permanent President. Although it didn't happen immediately, within two years of Carmela's tenure, Luxe returned to pre-scandal revenues. To this day she reigns as the hotel's President, and employees consistently report high confidence in her leadership and satisfaction in their work at the company.

::

Carmela used her voice to show reassurance, confidence, and credibility. Like Carmela, you can utilize your voice as a powerful tool to:

- Take listeners on a journey
- Display authority
- Disarm your audience
- Demonstrate approachability

Your listeners are (often subconsciously) clued into the subtleties of your voice,[9] paying attention to the emotion and confidence that is conveyed. Voice and speech specialist D'Arcy Webb asserts that a listener will determine if they like or don't like you *simply by the sound of your voice*. What they hear will dictate whether they would like to stay for more—or leave the room. Since your voice creates a range of impressions and can decide whether a person wants to be around you, it's important to be intentional about how you use it.

Mistakes People Make

The sound of your voice may not serve you or your listeners, particularly when you're nervous. This happens if you speak:

- Rapidly to get out of the spotlight
- Quietly (secretly hoping no one will hear you)
- In a low, creaky voice (also known as vocal fry)
- At a high pitch
- With sentences that end on a higher note than they begin, transforming your statements to questions (upspeak)
- In a monotone or mumble

By definition, your voice is the sound produced in the larynx and emitted from your mouth. This definition makes "using your voice" sound like a simple process. But in reality, D'Arcy explains how your voice is a complex instrument that is impacted by your posture, your breath, your facial expressions, the tension in your mouth and jaw and, yes, even the opening of your mouth.

---

9 Huler, Scott. "Does Tone Speak Louder Than Words?" *Duke Magazine*, 18 Feb. 2014.

Five Aspects of Voice

Here are five elements you can tinker with to offset these problems and that can be used to captivate listeners:

1. **The pace** (or the rate) at which you speak your words is impacted by your:
   - Communication style. People who are analytical thinkers speak at a slower pace because they're deliberate with their words. On the other hand, people who easily share what is on their mind often speak at a fast pace. (See Chapter 6 for a checklist to help you determine which communication style represents you.)

   To do: Determine your default style and adapt to your listeners' needs.

   - Emotional state. A slower pace can indicate sadness or concern while a faster pace can indicate excitement or energy.

   To do: Map your emotional state to your intent.

2. **Volume** refers to how loudly or softly you speak to capture attention.

   To do: Raise your volume to display emotion including frustration, excitement, or a call to action.

3. **Pitch** represents how high or low the voice sounds.
   - Research shows lower voices are more credible in both the business and political worlds.[10] And interestingly, when women's sentences end on a low note, they are also considered more dependable.

   To Do: Focus on ending your sentences low.

   - High pitch happens when you are nervous, and your vocal cords tighten

   To Do: Breathe to relax your vocal cords.

10 "New Research Finds There May Be a 'Million Dollar Voice' for CEOs." *Duke Fuqua Insights*, 17 Apr. 2013, https://www.fuqua.duke.edu/duke-fuqua-insights/ceo-million-dollar-voice.

4. **Intonation** references the musical flow of the voice over the course of a sentence or more.
   - Your listeners want to hear a musical flow to stay engaged with what you are saying. When intonation is missing, you sound monotone and your listeners tune you out.

   To Do: Create intonation using the strategies listed in Chapter 3.

5. **Enunciation** is clearly forming each word.
   - This is important for those who drop the endings of words, i.e., saying plannin' instead of planning. This is common among certain dialects like United States Southerners or some dialects in the United Kingdom and is further complicated when you speak at a fast pace or when English is not your first language.

   To Do: Speak slowly and clearly, emphasizing each word so people can understand you.

How to Combat Common Problems

Problem	Solution
Quick pace	Pause between each point. (see Chapter 1)
Slow pace, quiet or monotone	Practice energy strategies. (see Chapter 2)
Vocal fry or high squeaky voice	Relax your body, particularly focusing on your jaw, tongue, and your shoulders. Incorporate your abdomen when you speak by taking deep breaths.
Sentences sound like questions	End your sentences lower than you start. (See Exercise 2)
Mumbling	Intentionally enunciate each word. (See Exercise 4)

D'Arcy explains, "Speech work is 20% mechanics and 80% psychology. When you practice the exercises, so often, undiscovered emotions rise up and are unleashed." Examining your self-talk as well as your nervous system (see Chapters 10 and 11) can improve your vocal attributes.

Why Voices Go Awry

Vocal fry and upspeak are two characteristics that are common among young women. Upspeak is ending a sentence in a higher tone as if you are asking a question. Some women train themselves—both voluntarily and involuntarily—to use upspeak in certain situations to avoid being considered "bossy" or "bitchy." This illustrates the double bind women face when communicating. If they use a decisive tone, they are perceived as competent but not likable, and if they use an approachable voice, they're considered likable but not competent.[11]

Elizabeth Holmes, a Stanford dropout in her twenties, had a clear objective: she wanted to be powerful. Her innovative proposal to diagnose a wide range of medical conditions with a single drop of blood combined with her unique presence, captivated investors and the media alike. Elizabeth channeled Steve Jobs' black turtleneck fashion and spoke in an unnaturally deep voice, which experts later agreed was not her natural tone. It turns out her voice was just one of many deceptive aspects of her life; three years after Forbes named Elizabeth the youngest and wealthiest self-made female billionaire, she was indicted for fraud, shuttered her company, and reportedly is now millions of dollars in debt.

Vocal fry is the low, gravelly voice popularized by the Kardashians and actress Zooey Deschanel. Theories range about why people—mostly women—use vocal fry. Some think these traits emerge when women feel insecure and unconsciously mirror those around them in an attempt to "fit in." In a similar vein, vocal fry appears more often among peer groups, signifying that they are part of the same "tribe."[12]

---

11 "Infographic: The Double-Bind Dilemma for Women in Leadership" *Catalyst Research*, 2 Aug. 2018.

12 Madill, Cate. "Keep an Eye on Vocal Fry — It's All about Power, Status and Gender." *The Conversation*, 14 Nov. 2015.

A Deep Pitch

What's favorable about a deep voice? Deeper voiced CEOs manage larger companies, make more money, and enjoy longer tenures.[13] Also notable: voters prefer politicians with lower voices to those with a higher tone.[14] Ending your sentences in a lower tone also helps you combat upspeak, sound credible, and state your recommendations as declarations.

You can practice speaking sentences assertively and avoiding upspeak by practicing Exercise 2, "Speak Up, Dammit." This exercise involves making a statement followed by pounding your fist on a hard surface while saying, "dammit." This action shifts your statement from, "We may want to take this topic offline?" to "We may want to take this topic offline, dammit!"

Voice in Virtual Environments

Since we physically see less in a virtual environment, and also absorb fewer visual cues, the role that your voice plays is crucial. As a result, your energy, pauses, enunciation, and breath matter even more when you are talking on the phone or on Zoom.

What Everyone Can Do to Improve Their Voice

1. Recognize your vocal strengths and problem areas.
2. Practice. As D'Arcy says, your voice pattern is something "you've done for a long time. You have to practice just like you have to practice anything."
3. Speak from your core rather than using just your throat.
4. Relax. Notice tension and breathe to release it.

"When we speak effectively, we're making music."

D'ARCY WEBB, *The Speech Diva*

13 Davis, Nicola. "Deep Male Voices Evolved to Intimidate Men, Not Attract Women." *The Guardian*, 26 Apr. 2016.

14 Klofstad, Casey A., et al. "Sounds like a Winner: Voice Pitch Influences Perception of Leadership Capacity in Both Men and Women." *The Royal Society*, 14 Mar. 2012.

EXERCISES

Exercise 1: Vocal Assessment

What: Assess the effectiveness of your voice.

Why: Knowing your baseline vocal style will help you prioritize which aspects of your voice to improve.

How: Audio record conversations, phone calls, or meetings using your smartphone, then listen to the recordings. What do you notice? Which behaviors are more effective than you imagined them to be? Which behaviors need more development?

Rank the effectiveness of your voice on a scale of 1 (not effective) to 5 (most effective):

Rank the following vocal attributes on a scale of 1 to 5 and explain why you chose each score:

- Pace (speaking slowly or quickly)
- Volume (speaking softly or loudly)
- Pitch (speaking in a high tone or low tone)
- Intonation (musical flow of your voice over the course of a sentence)
- Enunciation (emphasizing specific words or phrases)

....

Exercise 2: "Speak Up, Dammit"

What: Practice stating a recommendation in a clear, affirmative manner.

Why: Women often share their opinions by ending their sentence in a higher tone than they started. This makes their statement sound like a question or upspeak. As a result, their opinions are not always taken seriously.

How: 1. Think of opinions you need to share.

Examples include:
- "My plan and budget are on target."
- "Let's review the financials."
- "We may want to take this topic offline."

2. State your opinion while holding your hand in the shape of a fist. As you end your sentence, slam your fist on the table or desk in front of you while saying, "dammit." In doing this, your statement shifts from, "We may want to take this topic offline?" to "We may want to take this topic offline, dammit!"
3. Record and listen to the different ways you make these statements.

Pro tip: When it's time to speak during a meeting, (please) eliminate the fist-slam and the spoken, "dammit"!

Exercise 3: "I Didn't Say I Kissed My Brother"

What: Practice changing the meaning of a statement based on which word you emphasize.

Why: When we are nervous or distracted, we can miss an opportunity to use our voice to impart meaning.

How:
1. Use either the sentence, "I didn't say I kissed my brother" or "I didn't say she stole the money."
2. Speak each sentence out loud three or more times, emphasizing a different word each time you say it.

   Examples:
   - I didn't SAY I kissed my brother
   - I didn't say I KISSED my brother
   - I didn't say I kissed my BROTHER.
3. Note how you can use emphasis to change the meaning of your content.

Exercise 4: Enunciate, Articulate, Exaggerate

What: A musical-preparation exercise to create clarity and crispness.

Why: When we are nervous and speak quickly, we can rush through our content or mumble our words. This exercise helps us to remember the importance of making each word count.

How: 1. State the following words clearly and crisply:

The lips, the teeth, the tip of the tongue.
The lips, the teeth, the tip of the tongue.
Articulate, Enunciate, Exaggerate, Tah!

Exercise 5: Convey Emotion

What: An exercise to practice how your tone can convey emotion.

Why: Our voice is an effective way to demonstrate urgency, excitement, empathy, and other emotions that move people to action.

How:

1. Read the following statements out loud:

   "My door is always open."
   "We did not make our numbers this quarter. It's time to double down and focus."
   "The client loved our proposal. They are ready to move forward."

2. Now infuse each of these statements with a specific emotion. For example, "My door is always open" can be stated sincerely or disingenuously.

   Or "The client loved our proposal. They are ready to move forward," can be stated with excitement or with trepidation.

3. Identify a statement you need to make in an upcoming meeting or conversation. Determine the emotion you want to convey and how to say your statement in a way that meets your goal.

CHAPTER 5

Body

Felicity was thrilled; her hard work was paying off. She had spent the last eight years as an architect in Indonesia taking advantage of their construction growth. Her projects focused on green design, which appealed to her because it was a hot new field. More than anything, she wanted to prove to Mr. Adams, her sexist high school calculus teacher, that a woman could be successful in a math-focused career.

Felicity had already earned a local reputation as a go-to architect for sustainable design and she was now focused on becoming recognized on a more global level. To meet her goal, she attended networking events and sought out opportunities to speak to community groups, students—anywhere and anything that would provide more exposure. Finally, her dream scenario arrived: she was asked to speak at a large architecture conference about her firm's sustainability projects. She was thrilled.

As exciting as it was, the thought of speaking to 4,000 peers was also terrifying. Up to this point, the largest group she had presented to was 100 people. And now 4,000? This was the opportunity of a lifetime.

To prepare, she carefully curated the content, architectural plans, and images she wanted to share. Then she spent hours scouring videos of speakers—mostly TED Talks—online. With a meticulous eye, Felicity noted their movement, gestures, and dramatic pauses.

She incorporated each speaker's best attributes when rehearsing her talk. She moved across the stage like the first speaker, gestured like the second, and paused like the third. She studied and rehearsed for weeks.

Finally, the big day arrived. Felicity's stomach was all butterflies due in equal parts to excitement and nerves. After having her makeup done and hair professionally styled, she felt confident and prepared.

In what felt simultaneously like one minute AND six hours later, she walked purposefully into the theater, one stiletto in front of the other. She reached the center of the stage, planted her body, and then started with, "We - have made - massive advancements - in the field - of - green - architecture." She punctuated each word with fully extended arms.

On stage, she felt courageous. She was speaking to more than 4,000 peers—and she was primed. At the end of the presentation, Felicity felt exuberant and relieved. She did it. Success!

Or was it?

Later, as she reviewed the video, she couldn't believe her own eyes. Her movements looked mechanical. Her gestures appeared orchestrated and produced—not at all natural. None of the behaviors she had used were authentically hers; they were a composite of numerous speakers that resulted in an overzealous and awkward delivery.

People remembered her presentation, but not necessarily in a good way. Some audience-goers felt empathy towards her; "That poor speaker appeared so nervous and uncomfortable."

In the end, her goal of presenting "perfectly" backfired. She missed the mark by trying too hard to adopt too many styles. She would have presented much better using her natural body language on stage.

Although her hyper-focus on body language was a flop, she continued to produce award-winning projects. And her doubting calculus teacher back home? He read about Felicity's architectural success when she was featured in the school newspaper as a VIP alum.

::

Like many of us, Felicity was unsure about how to use her body effectively when she speaks up. Yes, body language is important, but even more critical is to know that sometimes speakers place too much pressure on doing it "right." The downside of the pursuit of perfecting "authentic" body language is that sometimes speakers achieve the opposite and look unnatural.

In this chapter, we take a deep dive into body language and why it matters, but also why you shouldn't stress about it. And we'll identify how to stand, move, and use gestures that convey confidence and are natural to you.

Why is Body Language Important?

The way you move and gesture is important to your audience because—fun fact—it forms an impression of you in a split second. It's true. We automatically "judge books by their covers," explains psychology professor Nicolas Rule.[15] In fact, people tend to assess or judge others in a literal blink of an eye (about 100 milliseconds). Unfortunately, first impressions are hard to reverse, so your initial interaction with your listener is pivotal for your success.

The good news is that body language is only part of the picture. Your listeners also assess your facial expression, your warmth, and your energy. But because body language is a big part of the physical picture, we should aim towards getting it right.

The key themes to remember about body language are:

1. Be natural
2. Be symmetrical
3. Be welcoming

We'll apply these themes to confident standing positions, seated positions, movement, and gestures.

15 Rule, Nicholas. "Even Fact Will Not Change First Impressions." *Science Daily*, 14 Feb. 2014.

Natural Body Language

Stand Naturally

We spend the majority of our time hunched over a 4.5-inch screen with our shoulders rolled forward, "cavewoman" style. In addition to causing neck and back pain, this position does not look confident, or natural!

Confident standing poses start at the ground—literally. In yoga, this position is called mountain pose. It allows you to create a foundation that connects your feet to the ground to build strength throughout your body. This position is analogous to a tree where you are rooted and stabilized by the earth, and your body is elongated towards the sky. See Exercise 4 for specific steps to create a confident pose.

Standing naturally with your arms at your side makes you appear confident and welcoming. It also provides a neutral, non-distracting pose from which you can gesture to intentionally emphasize points. This position also prevents the viewer from being distracted by an awkward placement of your hands. (Hello, fig leaf)!

Symmetrical Body Language

Visualize a presenter standing at the front of the room. She has one leg crossed over the other. Or maybe she stands with one hip jutted out to the side, or she tilts her head as she speaks. What does her body language tell you about her?

Unfortunately, listeners involuntarily notice asymmetry and an imbalanced appearance, and it may tell them you're not confident or comfortable at the front of the room (*I know, you may not* feel *comfortable speaking up in front of a group but we don't want your body language to give it away*).

Asymmetrical positions can distract your listeners and prevent them from paying attention to what you're saying. In fact, evolution explains why our brains are wired to prefer symmetry: a "balanced" human body is considered to be more physically capable and, therefore, more likely to survive the attack of a predator. While you (probably) no longer need to worry about outrunning a bear, you can be sure the history of body language is rooted in symmetry.

Balanced body language may look confident to others but it may not feel natural to you. In fact, holding a symmetrical position might hurt or feel uncomfortable. Most new things do. Think about learning how to snowboard or going out for a jog the first time. These activities don't feel completely natural at first. With practice and time (and much bruising in the case of snowboarding), you will feel (more) comfortable standing in a balanced position. Exercise 3 tests this theory.

Welcoming Body Language

Have you ever noticed a woman standing at a networking event with her arms crossed in front of her chest or around her midsection? Or a man speaking to the room while playing with a ring on his finger, the keys in his pocket, or a pen in his hand? Or someone wagging their finger at the audience as they gesture? There is a common denominator of these positions: none of them make the listener feel welcome.

Let's look at what each behavior indicates:

Behavior:	Why It's Not Welcoming:	What You Can Do Instead:
Crossing your arms over your chest	This position looks defensive and closed off.	Hold an open body position with your arms at your side.
Crossing your arms around your middle	This position looks protective and closed off.	Hold an open body position with your arms at your side.

Playing with a ring, keys, a pen, a slide advancer, etc.	This position indicates the speaker is distracted and not completely focused on the listener.	If you are standing, hold your arms at your side. If you are seated, keep your hands flat on the table in front of you.
Wagging a finger or pointing towards your listeners	This is an accusatory position that puts your listeners on the defensive.	Use your entire hand rather than just your pointer finger (or any other finger!) when you emphasize a point.

Seated Body Language

Similar to a standing position, the goal when seated is to appear natural, symmetrical, and welcoming. To create this posture, make sure you are not hunched over (unnatural), that you are sitting up straight and not leaning to one side (asymmetrical) and remember, no elbows on the table (not welcoming). Instead, lean in to engage your listeners and, when you're in person, keep your hands where your listeners can see them. Like many nuances of body language, seeing someone's hands is important to your listeners on a subconscious level, so they know you aren't hiding anything.

Virtual Body Language

Body language can be tricky in virtual communication, but it's critical when on a video call. Some tips:

1. Camera angle matters. I have been on many a Zoom call and can say with certainty that there is nothing interesting about looking at a speaker's ceiling, nor is it a very flattering position as it also captures an "up the nostril" view. Angle wisely.
2. Sit up straight and have the camera capture as much of your upper body as possible so viewers can see your face and gestures.

3. Actions like nail biting, playing with jewelry, and hair twirling are amplified when virtual. These behaviors can indicate that you're nervous, which is not how you want to be perceived.

Gestures

No one knows what to do with their hands. It's even played out in the movie *Talladega Nights* where race car driver Ricky Bobby, portrayed by Will Farrell, is interviewed by a reporter. As he speaks post-race, Bobby's hands rise to within camera view and he says mid-interview, "I'm not sure what to do with my hands."[16]

A good rule of thumb is this: try not to overthink it. If you're worried about what to do with your hands, think back to the criteria for effective body language and ask, "Are my gestures natural? Are they symmetrical? Are they welcoming?"

So, what does this all mean? Let's break these down one at a time:

Natural Gestures

People worry that communicating with gestures can be too distracting. I often hear, "I'm Italian (or Middle Eastern or . . .) and I talk with my hands." Maybe you are accustomed to using repetitive gestures, and that motion may reflect your energy and passion. On the other hand, you may find you've trained yourself (or been trained) to show restraint, so you aren't gesturing enough. Exercise 5 will help you determine just how effective your gestures are.

If you follow the body language tips listed, you will punctuate your confident standing and seated positions with large, purposeful gestures. This creates interest and will emphasize your content to engage the audience. Many people are critical of their body language, but I find when speakers use natural gestures with intention, they become energized, and they capture the attention of their audience.

---

16 McKay, Adam, et al. *Talladega Nights: the Ballad of Ricky Bobby*. Sony Pictures Entertainment, 2006.

Examples of when to incorporate gestures include when you:

1. **Compare and contrast.** "Company A (while gesturing with your left hand outreached to the left side of your body) has seen tremendous growth while Company B (while gesturing with your right hand outreached to the ride side of your body) has been stagnant for the past year."
2. **Provide direction or describe a process.** "Our offices span from Los Angeles to New York" or "We start with the product team to determine the job description; then we obtain approval from finance; and finally, we work with HR to post the job," while indicating a range from one side of your body to the other.
3. **List action items.** "The city is focused on increasing: affordable housing, sustainable transportation, and afterschool care," while making distinct hand gestures from high to low or from one side to the other as you list each step.
4. **Provide emphasis.** Gestures are an ideal way to show scale, scope, growth, or reductions. For example, if you are talking about how profits have grown 200%, use large gestures to indicate the growth. This is particularly important when you are talking about large-scale numbers like hundreds of millions or billions of items.

Movement

Speaking while moving is hard. It doesn't feel natural, and many people resort to rocking or pacing while they present.

There is a spectrum of movement. On one extreme is pacing like a professor deep in thought or a tiger patrolling its cage. Some might argue that this motion is natural, "I pace when I think." That may be true, but the behavior is definitely not welcoming.

On the other extreme is looking like a deer in headlights or standing awkwardly, like a statue. This position doesn't look natural and when you appear uncomfortable, your audience becomes uncomfortable too.

Presentation coaches often recommend clients "move, then plant." The problem with this advice is people don't know how long to "plant" before they make their next move. In front of an audience, they get nervous and keep moving.

Instead, think of movement as an opportunity to interact with different parts of the room, remembering that the purpose is to transfer energy to each corner of the room.

For those who prefer an analogy, pretend your speaking space (or stage) is a baseball diamond. You stand on a base while you wait for the batter to hit the ball (this is the "plant") then you move to another base and repeat. In other words, you move, but it's not continual.

When you stand at the head of a table in a small conference room with no room for a baseball diamond, imagine moving between two bases. This is particularly effective if you move to a new spot when you start a new topic.

To recap: aim for natural and welcoming body language, as well as gestures and movement, but *don't sweat the details*. When you get the basics right, the culmination of your voice, eye contact, and facial expression are more important than the nuances of how you gesture.

EXERCISES

Exercise 1: Body Language Assessment

What: Evaluate videos to determine what others see.

Why: The way our body feels when we present is often different from how others perceive us.

How:

1. Use your phone or laptop to record video of yourself rehearsing a presentation or meeting update, one while you are standing and one while seated.
2. Watch both videos with the sound off so you can focus on your body language and gestures without getting distracted by the sound of your voice or your words.

   Remember to watch with self-compassion (as we discussed in Chapter 2, Connect).
3. What do you notice as you watch?

   How would you rate symmetry on a scale of 1 (not effective) to 10 (very effective)? Which behaviors contributed?
   - One leg crossed over the other
   - One or both hand(s) in your pocket(s)
   - Balanced "ready" position
   - Sitting symmetrical in your chair
   - One hip jutted out to the side or placing weight on only one leg
   - Arms crossed in front of your body

How would you rate how natural your body language looks on a scale of 1-10? Which behaviors contributed?
- Using gestures to make a point
- Gesturing while keeping your elbows glued to your sides vs. with your entire arm(s)
- Constant movement
- Intentional, natural-looking movement
- Appearing awkwardly rooted to the ground
- Appearing comfortably rooted to the ground

How would you rate how welcoming your body language looks on a scale of 1-10? Which behaviors contributed?
- Arms crossed in front of your body
- Moving around the space to connect with listeners
- Leaning in to connect
- Leaning back
- Your hands kept under the table
- Your hands resting on top of the table

Exercise 2: Identify a Role Model

What: Find a body language role model to help determine how you want to be perceived.

Why: Body language is tricky; it's hard for us to follow standard guidelines. It's easier to view someone who uses body language well and focus on replicating those behaviors.

How: 1. Identify someone who uses effective body language. This could be someone you know like a co-worker, neighbor, or someone you have observed like an actor or a speaker at a TED Talk.

2. Notice the behaviors s/he uses when standing, seated, and gesturing. Complete the following chart about this person's body language. The first line contains an example:

	Write Down Name of Body Language Role Model: ______________________	
Body Position:	**Behaviors:**	**Impression:**
Standing	Shoulders are back, tall posture, one hand is in pocket	Casually confident

Exercise 3: Cross Your Arms

What: An exercise to determine whether what you feel is consistent with what others see.

Why: Some of our habits feel good to us, like slouching, because we are used to hovering over a laptop or our phones. While slouching may feel natural to you, your observer (or boss) might disagree. Changing behaviors, like adopting a good standing or seated posture, can feel awkward. The point of this exercise is to determine if the awkwardness you feel is obvious to those observing you.

How: 1. Find a colleague, friend, or family member to watch as you:
   - Cross one arm over the other at chest height, as you normally would do.
   - Then cross your arms the "wrong" way by placing the opposite arm on top. Note: do not tell your observer which arm crossing is the "right" way and which is the "wrong" way.
2. Ask your observer which arm crossing is the "right" way. You may be surprised that even though the wrong way feels terrible to you, your observer may not notice how uncomfortable it feels. In fact, they may not be able to identify which is the right and wrong way.

Exercise 4: Improve Your Posture

What: Learn and practice the steps for developing effective posture.

Why: Good posture helps you appear confident and competent yet our society's tendency to hunch over phones and slouch in chairs means you may need to train or remind yourself how to create good posture.

How: 1. Plant your feet on the ground with your weight equally distributed hip-width apart.
2. Bend your knees slightly to stay fluid and to prevent locking up and looking awkward.
3. Elongate your body by imagining you have a string attached to the top of your head that is being pulled by a gentle giant. In this position, line your head over your shoulders, your shoulders over your hips, and your hips over your ankles.
4. Roll your shoulders back, and squeeze your shoulder blades together (imagine you are holding a pencil between your shoulder blades behind you).

5. Hold your arms straight down at your sides as if you are holding a can of paint in each hand. Slightly bend your elbows so you don't overextend your arm.
6. Stand in this position for 60 seconds. Like Exercise 3: Cross Your Arms, this position may feel uncomfortable. During this time, notice what feels awkward and see if you can breathe through the discomfort.

Pro Tip: Visualize people who display good body language to help you replicate good posture.

Exercise 5: Assess Your Gestures in Your "Natural Habitat"

What: Determine how effective your gestures truly are.

Why: People often misjudge what their gestures look like. Many assume they are distracting while others don't realize that one particular repetitive gesture is not additive.

How:

1. Record yourself talking at a virtual meeting, presentation, at the dinner table, or telling a story to friends (by propping up a smartphone or using an app like Zoom on your laptop).
2. Watch your recordings(s) with the sound off.
3. Assess your body language asking, "Do I . . . ":
   - Cross my arms in front of my body?
   - Gesture with my elbows glued to my sides?
   - Continually gesture?
   - Use gestures effectively to emphasize a point, to show size or scale, or to explain?

Exercise 6: Gesture Practice

What: An opportunity to practice gestures using prompts.

Why: Clients worry they don't know which gestures to do nor when to do them. This exercise will help you practice and find optimal times when presenting.

How:

1. Video-record yourself saying the following statements while using gestures to complement your material:
   - *Compare and contrast:* "Vendor A creates beautiful websites at a high cost. Vendor B's websites are simple and lower priced."
   - *List items:* "We will focus on the following markets: Detroit, Memphis, Houston, and Denver." Or "To launch the project, we need a product team, a marketing plan, and a sales strategy."
   - *Emphasis:* "Since 2019, we have quadrupled our sales." Or "This problem is infinitely larger than any of us imagined."
2. Watch the videos without sound. Note whether your gestures are effective at demonstrating comparisons, quantifying, or emphasizing. If you are not sure, re-record with more distinct, exaggerated gestures and compare this version with your first recording.

Pro Tip: Show your videos to a colleague or a friend to get their assessment of your gestures' effectiveness. Like Exercise 3: Cross Your Arms and Exercise 4: Improve Your Posture, how your body feels may starkly differ from how it looks.

CHAPTER 6

Goals

Jasmin was fired up. As someone who perpetually sought new and thrilling experiences, the pandemic might have dampened her style. But she's an out-of-the-box thinker. Despite the hardships of COVID-19, she was motivated to pursue her passion: marketing for Escapade, a travel company focused on unique trips. On this particular spring morning she was excited about a team call to brainstorm virtual journeys tailored for quarantined customers. Creativity and adventures were Jasmin's two main loves; this was going to be fun.

Jasmin logged onto the call early, eager to get started. As she casually chatted with two colleagues on her team, she became distracted by the Bing! Bing! Bing! announcing new attendees joining the call. She had not realized her boss's boss plus two people from finance, a member of the legal team, and three people whose names she did not recognize would also be on the call. Yikes—this was now a much bigger deal. The unfamiliar faces—and number of people present—began to dampen Jasmin's spirit. Now she felt the need to impress this larger group, not just communicate her ideas. She brushed off her discomfort when Sonya, her beloved manager, started the meeting by stating, "Today's objective is to explore inventive ideas for staying relevant, increasing our market share, and creating the best damn customer experience in these unprecedented times. Let's do this!"

Sonya and her manager began the meeting discussing virtual concerts and which popular talent to target. They lobbed ideas back and forth while Jasmin eagerly waited to contribute. Twelve minutes into the call, Jasmin finally spoke up. "In addition to concerts, I'd like to suggest activities that our customers can do. Specifically, virtual games and competitions." She sensed the participants were engaged, so she continued explaining how to implement her ideas. Yet as she kept talking, she realized, "You're babbling. Shut up! You're no longer making sense." Jasmin paused, not sure what to do next. Luckily her team jumped in with additional ideas about virtual travel, sporting events, and cooking lessons.

After the meeting, Sonya sent Jasmin a link to the call recording with a note, "Will you review the video to make sure we capture every suggestion?" Jasmin was happy to own this task. She could not wait to see all the ideas captured in one document.

That afternoon, Jasmin clicked the link to the recording of the meeting and realized that in addition to collecting the innovative ideas that were suggested, she would need to listen to herself blather along during the initial part of the meeting. She dreaded reliving that moment but clicked 'Play' anyway.

When she heard her voice, it took her breath away. She felt her blood run cold. Ugh. She hated how she sounded. Her voice seemed so . . . unfamiliar. So different. But as she continued to listen, she noticed something else: she was making perfect sense. Her ideas flowed. What felt like excessive chatter at the time was actually a complete explanation of each idea she had mentioned. "Wow," she thought, "I was sure I was rambling, but I actually sounded coherent." She was so distracted by this unexpected discovery that she'd forgotten to document the specific experience ideas. She scrolled back to the beginning to listen again.

This time, she had acclimated to the sound of her voice but she noticed something new. She said, "um" or "like" at least once during every sentence. How had she not noticed this before? Jasmin was shocked that she used so many filler words. She was embarrassed but determined to eliminate them from her speech patterns.

Now that she knew she had a distracting habit, Jasmin sought my advice to determine how to become a filler-free speaker. We landed on a three-pronged approach: 1. Commit to listening to "ums" and "likes" as she talked, 2. Replace filler words with pauses and 3. Ask her trusted colleague, Luis, to hold her accountable by pointing out her "ums" and "likes" during their daily conversations.

Jasmin was amazed that with the simple assessment of listening to her call—twice—she was able to identify speaking imperfections she hadn't realized existed. Without this knowledge, she never would have worked on her communication skills. Although it took time, regular practice, and Luis's support, she was able to eliminate most of her filler words and speak with more confidence.

::

Think about your last communication. How did it go? Is your perception accurate? What would your best friend say about it? Likely, your feelings about your communication differ from how others perceive it. Our self-evaluation is altered by how we process, select, and interpret situations. Your best friend, your mother, and your coworker each interpret the same situation differently. You don't have accurate insight about how you are perceived because your understanding is clouded by past experience and self-doubt. Our bias towards the negative is an evolutionary trait that helped our ancestors stay alert when their life depended on avoiding threats. As it turns out, our brains haven't evolved all that much since then. We often aren't aware of our blind spots.

::

Kristina faced this situation when she conducted televised interviews for a college broadcast journalism class. Before and during the interviews her predominant feeling was: "I'm not prepared." Even after extensive research, careful crafting of interview questions, and twelve interviews under her belt, she never felt fully ready.

When Kristina showed the recorded clips to a professional television anchor, the anchor said she was too soft-spoken. Kristina had never considered this about herself and had never heard this feedback. Instead, Kristina had been overly concerned about her preparation, which was actually spot on. Kristina might never have known that she comes across as quiet if she had not asked for feedback from a person experienced in the field.

::

There are many times when we incorrectly assume—or don't know—how we are perceived. It happens to the best of us. To improve our Speak Up skills, we need to identify our blind spots. You have already started this process by conducting assessments through the exercises in each of the prior chapters.

The next step is to ask trusted colleagues, friends, or mentors how they assess your style. Since that is a broad question, we'll make it easier by pinpointing your optimal communication style. Exercises 1 and 2 give you prompts for identifying speakers you admire and the qualities that make them interesting to you.

In Exercise 3, you will compare your assessments with the qualities you admire in others. This is the information you will share with your colleagues, friends, or mentors in Exercise 4. Based on what you see and what your supportive network shares with you, the final step is to prioritize three areas to improve in Exercise 5.

Speak Up Role Models

Do you remember when you were in first grade and looked up to your teacher? You loved the way she smiled at you. You loved the sundress she wore and how she gently reigned from a sturdy, wooden chair above your class as you and your classmates sat crisscross applesauce on the faded blue carpet, gazing lovingly up at her. She read a chapter from *Narnia* in her kind, sing-songy voice and you just simply wanted to BE her.

As children we naturally identify role models to learn how to behave and to inspire who we want to become. It's no surprise that role models are beneficial. Yet when we think of the term "role model," we envision someone who serves as an inspiration to kids or teens. Rarely do we consider that adults need role models too, but research shows that a mentor impacts both how an adult perceives herself as well as how others perceive her.[17]

Previous chapters showed you how to prioritize the areas you'd like to improve. The next step is to identify role models who will serve as both an inspiration and an archetype for how to speak up.

My Speak Up role model is a former colleague named Bronwyn. She inspires me because she elects to play big and share her voice—even in the most nerve-wracking situations.

::

When Bronwyn was in her 20s, she worked for a boutique public relations agency whose cornerstone client was Nosh, a consumer packaged goods business. Three years into the relationship, Nosh encountered a major financial obstacle. Sales had been slow and Nosh was laying people off in droves.

Bronwyn knew her bread-and-butter account was on the line. She needed to act, and fast. She scheduled a meeting with the CEO to unveil an out-of-the box strategy—an innovative high-risk media plan to reshape how customers perceived Nosh.

Bronwyn knew Nosh's CEO Jocelyn, a buttoned up, conservative leader (whose job was vulnerable), would not be easily won over. Bronwyn needed to exhibit the confidence she felt around her big idea.

As the day of the meeting approached, Bronwyn donned her favorite power outfit and channeled her 1980s rockstar idol, David Lee Roth (the energetic lead singer of Van Halen), as she strutted directly into the CEO's office.

Bronwyn launched into her presentation by painting a bold picture of how to secure press around Nosh's repositioning. Jocelyn watched intently, not saying a word, so Bronwyn took this as a sign to continue.

---

17 Brown, M. E., and L. K. Treviño. "Do Role Models Matter? An Investigation of Role Modeling as an Antecedent of Perceived Ethical Leadership." *APA PsycNet*, 2014.

As she completed the presentation, Bronwyn felt cautiously optimistic. She waited for Jocelyn's response.

Jocelyn sat frozen for a minute. To Bronwyn, it felt like an eternity. "Well . . . " she began slowly. "I think this plan has legs. It's not what I expected, but I think we should talk through potential next steps." By playing big, Bronwyn not only saved the business, she convinced Jocelyn to increase the scope and the budget for the revised PR campaign. She saved her job and her agency's biggest account.

::

If you asked Bronwyn about her role models, she would tell you she is inspired by the "high kicks delivered by a killer front man on stage. Inspired not by choreography—but by instinct. By **rock**." To this day she has never met David Lee Roth, but she channels his energy before important meetings. It provides her with strength and vitality, and helps her feel motivated to show up with confidence.

As for me? I, in turn, channel Bronwyn before *my* high-stakes situations.

But here's the cool thing. Your role model can be someone you've never met. Or it can be a person you know, someone whose behaviors you've actually witnessed, as Bronwyn is to me. Or perhaps they are symbolic—real people you don't know like Greta Thunberg, Malala Yousafzai, Megan Rapinoe. Or they can even be a fictional character like Wonder Woman or *Scandal*'s Olivia Pope, the crisis manager who "fixes" political complications and controversies.

The idea of learning new behaviors simply by observing is backed by the social learning theory, which explains the power of modeling in changing behaviors.[18]

Another way to identify your Speak Up mentor is to compile behaviors and characteristics of various idols to create a role model persona. Beyoncé created Sasha Fierce, an alternate persona who represents the confident, sexy, assertive characteristics that she wanted to channel on stage.

---

18 Bandura, Albert. *Social Learning Theory*. Englewood Cliffs, N.J: Prentice Hall, 1977.

So, start thinking about the people who inspire you when you observe them. What behaviors do they display that you want to emulate?

EXERCISES

Exercise 1: Speak Up Role Models

What: Identify people who demonstrate your ideal speaking qualities.

Why: Having Speak Up role models provides a North Star (a guide), and increases your ability to improve your communication skills.

How: Brainstorm the names of people that you consider to be excellent communicators. These could be people you know (your boss, your relative, a neighbor) or that you've never met (the CEO of your company, someone you've seen on TV or online). In your Speak Up journal, write down any and all speakers you admire.

....

Exercise 2: Speak Up Role Model Characteristics

What: Identify the behaviors your role models demonstrate.

Why: Knowing the specific characteristics or behaviors is important to know what to emulate and cultivate.

How: Think about the specific characteristics your mentors possess.

1. Identify the impressions your role models create e.g., confident, bad-ass, strong, personable, credible, charismatic, good storytellers, funny, etc. In your journal, create a table like the one listed below and fill out the Speak Up role model names and impressions.

2. Dive into the specific behaviors that create those impressions. Make sure to include their Pause, Connect, Energy, Voice, and Body characteristics.

   Here is a table you can recreate in your journal. Although this table shows only two role models, in your journal you should list as many as you have.

Name of Speak Up Role Model #1:	Impressions They Create:	Characteristics of:
Example: Kamala Harris	Strong and warm	Pause: at regular intervals to emphasize her points
		Connect: direct eye contact and a warm smile
		Energy: strong passion and contagious energy
		Voice: clear without filler words
		Body: impressive posture
Name of Speak Up Role Model #2:		
		Pause:
		Connect:
		Energy:
		Voice:
		Body:

Exercise 3: Self-Assessment

What: Compare your assessment with your role models' behaviors.

Why: To build your communication skills, it's helpful to know where you want to go and compare that to where you are now.

How:

1. Revisit your answers to Question 1 in the Intro chapter to recall your Speak Up goal. Which behaviors will create the biggest impact towards meeting your communication goals?
2. Review the chapter assessment exercises (Exercise 1) in Chapters 1-5. What do you notice as you review all five assessments?
3. Compare your assessment with your role model's behaviors. Where are you aligned? Where do you differ?

Impression I Want to Create:	Specific Behavior My Role Model Uses:	Specific Behavior I Use:
Confident	Pause: Intentionally to create impact.	Say "um" too much.
	Connect: __________	
	Energy: __________	
	Voice: __________	
	Body: __________	

Exercise 4: Ask a Friend

What: An activity to uncover your blind spots.

Why: It's important to get other people's perspective because they view us differently than we view ourselves.

How: Ask other people to complete the chart below to learn how they view your communication skills.

Impression I Want to Create:	Specific Behaviors Needed to Create This Impression:	How I Assess Myself:	How My Manager / Colleague / Mentor Perceives Me:
Credible	Pause: To remove filler words	I say, "um" and "like" too often	She agrees with my assessment
	Connect: Hold direct eye contact	I look up to think	She thinks my connection is good
	Energy: __________		
	Voice: __________		
	Body: __________		

Exercise 5: Prioritize Your Goals

What: Identify what areas to improve.

Why: It's important to have a plan in order to improve.

How: Based on what you learn, what three areas do you want to prioritize improving? Write your three priority areas in your journal.

Note: One of your three priorities should focus on the pivotal Speak Up behaviors: pause, connect or energy.

1. ____

2. ____

3. ____

CHAPTER 7
Audience

When Stacy was nine years old, she was diagnosed with Type 1 diabetes. The diagnosis required periodic visits to pediatrician and endocrinologist offices, which were made more complicated by her family's frequent moves. Stacy has vivid memories of her father calling physicians trying to coordinate the transfer of her medical records to new doctors in each hometown.

After college Stacy learned about MedSoft, a company that digitized medical records to make it easier for patients to access their information from any doctor, anywhere. MedSoft's vision was personal to her, and she eagerly applied for a position marketing medical record software. She had landed her dream job, except for one thing—MedSoft's Marketing Director, Marq.

Marq was a brilliant guy with a healthy ego to match. He graduated from an Ivy League school with a degree in classical philosophy. Marq believed that in order to be impactful in business, one needed a deep knowledge of the literary classics, even when the business at hand was to promote software to physicians.

When he would meet with his marketing team, Marq harkened Socrates, discussed Descartes, and read lines from Shakespeare plays without directly connecting those philosophies to the current goal. The result? Confused team members who could draw no link between his oration and medical record software.

Meanwhile, Stacy's team was tasked with preparing a strategic marketing plan despite having received zero guidance from Marq. Their proposal looked like a menu of ideas: too many options and no real strategy. The plan was to be presented to MedSoft's executive team at the end of the week.

Two days before the executive presentation, Marq held a team meeting where he confidently stood at the front of the room reciting lines from Shakespeare's Julius Caesar:

"There is a tide in the affairs of men
Which, taken at the flood, leads on to fortune;
Omitted, all the voyage of their life
Is bound in shallows and in miseries."

Stacy watched quietly, slack-jawed and stumped. As Marq spoke, she surreptitiously glanced at her colleagues, gauging whether they were tracking what he said or if they were as lost as she felt. As always, Marq finished his lecture with just minutes left on the clock.

"What exactly should we do with this information?" Stacy asked.

Marq looked over the glasses perched on his nose, sighed, and responded in an exasperated tone: "Let this passage inspire you!"

"Okay," Stacy stated in a tone barely masking her annoyance. "Um, how does this relate to marketing MedSoft?"

"That, my friends, is your job to figure out! Share your plan by the end of day," Marq sang as he strolled out of the room.

Marq's team was dumbfounded. They remained in the room, trying to decipher his message and figure out what to do next.

"So, what do we do now?" "What was he saying?" "How does this help promote our software?" the team members asked over one another.

"Anyone here a Shakespeare major?" Stacy quipped.

"Oh, I was," Cristina responded with equal sarcasm.

They decided to piece together what they could recall from Marq's speech. The process resembled a crime scene investigation.

"There was something about miseries."

"Yes, and a tide and a voyage."

With these keywords, they searched the internet to find the entire Julius Caesar passage. Once they found it, they were equally stuck. What did it mean? They batted around interpretations of the speech. At one point, Cristina rolled her eyes and said, "I cannot believe we are spending THIS amount of time researching how Julius Caesar relates to medical software."

As she finished, Stacy exclaimed, "I've got it! I googled the passage and the words 'business context.' The passage means 'when we are in a position of flood—or opportunity—we need to act or else we wind up miserable.' If that's the case, I think Marq is telling us to act now!"

"That makes sense," Cristina responded cautiously. "So, after wasting hours trying to interpret Marq's instructions, I suppose we should propose a plan for a bold launch and recommend getting the materials out ASAP?"

The team agreed.

"Wouldn't this have been simpler if Marq had said, in plain English, what he wanted us to do?"

The team nodded. They worked late into the night as Stacy's blood sugar rose, requiring her to inject additional insulin. They submitted their plan to Marq just before midnight.

Two days later, Marq presented the plan to the executive team, who responded positively. While the marketing team should have been ecstatic about the executive's approval, they were exhausted and frustrated by the opaque instructions, the time it took to decipher Marq's communication, and the toll this unnecessarily stressful situation had taken on Stacy and her team's mental and physical health. They were left with no gas in their tanks to do the meaningful work: connect with doctors to promote MedSoft.

::

Marq's passion for classical literature would find a better outlet on a stage or in a university auditorium. Although he sincerely believes ancient philosophy ties into business, he's been unable to build a bridge between his literature references and marketing for MedSoft.

As a result, he provides little relevance to those in the room, and in this case, has let down the members of his team.

Sadly, he's not the only businessperson who miscommunicates his perspective or passion, and is therefore oblivious to how it impacts those around him.

Gia, a young, energetic client of mine, had the same problem. She eagerly contributed during meetings, but focused only on her objectives. When others spoke, she diverted the conversation back to her agenda. As you can imagine, the team was tired—*really tired*—of Gia's self-centered style.

When we reviewed recordings of her team meetings, Gia was surprised how much time she spent talking about her projects. It finally registered that in order to make headway, and for her to feel heard, she needed to tie her recommendations to her team members' interests.

During the next meeting, Gia changed her style in two ways. First, she listened more and talked less. Second, she incorporated her ideas into her team members' initiatives. Gia was amazed at the response. Her colleagues were interested in working together. She had made a simple pivot, and instead of hammering the team with her ideas, she began to integrate them into the collective conversation. In other words, she learned to make more room at the table.

Why Are We Self-Centered?

We all communicate our passions and perspectives to some degree. It's hard to avoid since our thoughts are biased towards what appeals or relates to us. A Duke University psychology and neuroscience professor discusses this phenomenon in his article, "It's Not Your Fault — Your Brain is Self-Centered,"[19] where he shares research that shows we prioritize "self" in our thoughts.[20]

As the research indicates, most people naturally lean toward a communication style that focuses on topics that meet their personal needs

---

19 Yin, Shouhang, et al. "Automatic Prioritization of Self-Referential Stimuli in Working Memory." *Psychological Science*, Mar. 2019.

20 Duong, Yen. "It's Not Your Fault -- Your Brain Is Self-Centered." *Duke Today*, 13 Mar. 2019.

or interests. In business, this can mean centering the conversation on information that illustrates or validates their work or their accomplishments. And yet communicating this way, from your self-centered brain (remember, it's not your fault!), will not meet listeners' needs. They will become bored or fed up. This is even more important in a virtual environment where your listeners may be multitasking and, as a result of your self-indulgence, might tune you out.

What's in It for Me

To remedy self-centeredness, *consciously* think externally about your listeners' needs. "What's in It for Me?" (WIIFM) is a term that refers to our natural, egocentric tendency to prioritize ourselves. Ironically, even though WIIFM stands for What's in It for *Me*, WIIFM (in business) is the acronym used to remind ourselves of the importance of prioritizing the needs of our *audience*.

Your goal as a speaker is to address your listeners' WIIFM. This is more than just an empathetic communication style; thinking about your listeners is also the method for gaining buy-in and earning respect.

An example of why this is important:

::

Charlie is a dedicated environmentalist and nonprofit Executive Director who has spent decades preserving the Amazon. Her nonprofit has lofty goals and needs to raise hundreds of thousands of dollars to protect indigenous people and the rainforest.

One of Charlie's board members organized a fundraiser in a wealthy community outside of New York City. She was excited to educate and inspire this philanthropic group of individuals.

On the night of the event in the impeccably decorated living room of a stately Tudor home, Charlie was introduced to a group of more than 50 well-heeled potential donors. She started by introducing the Amazon via slides projected onto a large screen TV. The images were stunning, and Charlie thoroughly explained what each image represented. After 20 minutes, the room got antsy. Legs crossed, and then uncrossed. People shifted in their chairs. Some snuck to the back of the room to refill their glass of wine. Others surreptitiously glanced at their phones. Yet Charlie continued to talk.

About 35 minutes into her speech, she noticed the room starting to quietly talk to each other. She was losing them and she hadn't even reached her "ask" to fund a new program that would cost well into the six figures.

By the time she unveiled the new program and explained why it mattered, as well as how much it would cost, only a quarter of the room was listening. She left the evening with just 10% of her fund-raising goal.

::

Where did Charlie go wrong? Well, she didn't do her research. If she'd asked about her audience before the event, she would have learned that this room was very knowledgeable about environmental issues. They cared about the Amazon, and they already knew most of the information Charlie had shared. The philanthropic room wanted to hear how Charlie's program was different, and how their donations would create an impact. If she had spent 30 minutes focused on understanding the audience before her presentation, she would have had a much different outcome.

So, what does this mean for *your* communication? As you prepare to contribute at a meeting, think about who will be in the room.

Ask yourself, "What does my listener need to hear from me?" This is a broad but useful question to orient yourself to your listeners' needs.

Here are three categories of questions you can ask to learn more about your audience, which helps you tailor your content to their needs:

1. Broad context

This information orients you to the room and helps you prioritize your focus and how to prepare. For example, if five people plan to attend a meeting but only two people are responsible for approving your suggested next steps, you should spend your preparation time focused on the two who are most relevant.

Also consider the business context. How is your information important to the company? To the business unit? To the people in the meeting?

Exercise 2 provides a list of questions for you to answer when you prepare for a Speak Up opportunity.

2. Knowledge-based

Knowledge-based questions determine what your audience already knows, what type of information they need, and how they will apply it. For example, if the decision maker knows the background of the problem, you should spend very little time sharing the backstory and focus your time on the plan and next steps. This applies to Charlie when she described the rainforest. Had she answered the questions listed in Exercise 2 before her talk, she would have better met her philanthropic audience's needs.

If your meeting attendees don't need the full story, then that's easy: don't provide it! Often meetings are multi-purpose and not everyone in the meeting needs or cares about every topic. Either way, focus your content preparation on what your listeners need to know.

> If meeting attendees are unfamiliar with the background, ask yourself, "Do they need to know the complete story? Do they care?" If so, consider a short summary that covers the key highlights, sending information in advance, or holding a call before the meeting to get them up to speed.

3. Communication style

Each of us prefers to communicate, receive information, and make decisions in a particular way. For example, do you share your opinion readily, or ensure your ideas are fully baked before communicating? Do you speak from your gut, or research and document?

Knowing your communication biases and determining your communication preferences are important so you can make sure your listeners hear your points.

For example, let's imagine you are an analytical person who likes to nerd out on numbers and details. You'll likely want to present data and spreadsheets to your audience. But even if your listeners share your love for numbers, let's get real—they're busy and, like most people, they want the bottom line stated succinctly.

On the other hand, if you are a communicator who is excited to share a vision with storytelling, make sure your style matches your audience's overall interest in the big picture (or in examples that illustrate the message). If your audience prefers specifics, they may view the vision and stories as extraneous.

::

Sophie has spent much of her career working as a consultant at Big Four accounting firms. In other words, she's whip smart. In addition to the quality of her work, Sophie prided herself in her warm and likable personality. Imagine her surprise when she received feedback that her positive and bubbly disposition potentially undermined her credibility. This bit of criticism stung. Upon further reflection, and after more years of experience, Sophie now realizes her effervescent style is well received in her meeting with design leaders, but not so when she presents to more analytical types.

::

Exercise 1 provides an opportunity to answer these questions and more, and will better assess your communication preferences.

When I asked Geetha, an Agile coach, what advice she would give to women just starting out in their career, she said, "I wish I knew early on that people are different, and you cannot use just one communication style for everybody. Every situation, each person is different. Depending on if I give you an orientation or if I want you to act or I want you to think, my communication style needs to be different."

The bottom line? It's important to tailor what you say to *their* needs.

EXERCISES

Exercise 1: Self Analysis

What: Determine your communication preferences.

Why: Understanding your needs and predispositions illuminates biases you have around how you communicate information. This helps you identify how you can adapt your communication style to meet the needs of your listeners.

How: 1. Circle which characteristics best describe how you like to structure your information:

State the bottom line first	Provide a thorough explanation
Share my opinion readily	Make sure my ideas are fully baked, and ideally road-tested with a friend or someone I trust before sharing
Go with my gut	Research and document
Prefer to make decisions quickly	Prefer to make decisions carefully
Interrupt at times	Listen carefully
Focus on the possibility, vision, or reward	Focus on safety and risk

2. Circle which characteristics best describes what type of information you prefer:

Stories and anecdotes	Data
Colorful details and images	Graphs, tables, and charts
Testimonials	Research and documentation

- If your answers fall in one column, you likely need to "flex" to the other to truly meet the needs of your audience.

Plan how to adapt to different audiences so you can more readily share the type of information that is most useful to them.

Exercise 2: Analyze Them

What: Determine your listeners' communication preferences.

Why: Understanding their needs and preferences helps you determine what type of content to share, and how to do so to meet the needs of your listeners.

Broad context

- What are your listeners' roles?
- Who do they report to?
- Who is the decision maker(s)?
- What are the business priorities?
- What are the team's priorities?
- How does your information fit into the goals of those in the room?

Knowledge-based

- What do your listeners already know about the topic?
- What information do they need to know?
- Why do they care about the topic (or do they care about it)?
- How will they use this information?
- What could happen if they don't receive this information?
- What will happen when they do?

Communication style

Do your listeners:

State the bottom line	Provide a thorough explanation	Mix of both
Share opinions readily	Make sure ideas are fully baked, and ideally road-tested before sharing	Mix of both
Go with their gut	Research and document	Mix of both
Prefer to make decisions quickly	Prefer to make decisions carefully	Mix of both
Interrupt at times	Listen carefully	Mix of both
Focus on the possibility, vision, or reward	Focus on safety and risk	Mix of both

Circle which characteristics best describes what type of information your listeners prefer:

Stories and anecdotes	Data and spreadsheets	Mix of both
Colorful details, images, and videos	Graphs, tables, and charts	Mix of both
Testimonials	Research and documentation	Mix of both

When people ask, "What do I do if I don't know the answers to all these questions?" I tell them to get creative. Be detectives. Look for clues.

For example, if you have interacted with your listeners by email, how much detail do they provide? What is the focus on their content?

If you haven't interacted with them, can you find someone who has? If not, identify someone who represents your target audience, someone in the same type of role or same type of company.

Exercise 3: Summarize Your Audience with a Table Diagram

What: Create an illustration that summarizes your listeners and their needs.

Why: Having a visual representation of your listeners is a useful way to keep your audience's needs in mind when planning your communication.

How:

1. On an 8x10 inch piece of paper, draw a table from the aerial view i.e., looking down at it.
2. Draw one circle for each audience member who will attend your Speak Up event. This circle represents your audience member's chair.
3. Above each circle, write the participant's name or initials.
4. Within each circle, write how they like to receive information. Do they prefer to hear the headline or the background and all the details? Do they want decisions made quickly or do they prefer a well-vetted response?
5. Below each circle, write what type of information they like to receive. Do they prefer to review raw data? See graphs or tables? Hear stories? See pictures or visuals?
6. On the table in front of each listener, draw a square representing a plate. (It's a modern plate, ok?) The plate represents the type of information your listeners will "consume."
7. Write on each plate what you will do to adapt to each listener. For example, for the financial analyst who values avoiding risk, you might write, "Highlight how to mitigate risk."

8. On the back side of the paper answer the following questions:
   - How much do your listeners know about the information you plan to share?
   - What do they think about your ideas?
   - What will they do with this information?
   - What will happen if they don't receive this information?

Exercise 4: Summarize Your Audience in a Chart

What: Fill out a table to represent your listeners and their needs.

Why: Seeing a table summarizing your listeners' preferences is a useful way to keep your audience's needs in mind when planning your communication. Note: this exercise can be done in addition to, or instead of, Exercise 3.

How: 1. Complete the following table:

Name of Person at Your Speak Up Event	How Do They Prefer Receiving Information?	What Type of Information Do They Like to Receive?	How Will You Adapt to Them?

EXERCISE 5:
Orient Towards the Audience

What: Identify questions to ask at the beginning of each speaking moment.

Why: By default, we think of ourselves first. Identifying questions that orient you to the audience will help you keep their needs in mind when you communicate.

How: 1. Craft one or two questions to ask yourself about your audience before each Speak Up opportunity.

Examples include: "What is most important to my audience right now?" or "How do they like to receive their information?"

Craft your questions here:

1 ____

2. ____

CHAPTER 8

Structure

Jana is an energetic, inventive business prodigy. At just 26 years old, she founded Cheekin, a rapidly growing company that makes a plant-based chicken substitute. As the founder of an innovative company, she regularly receives media interview requests. Against her team's advice, Jana never prepares. She simply shows up and starts talking.

On this particular morning, Jana strode into Cheekin's lobby, her frenetic energy matching the dizzying colors of her flowy dress. She was thrilled to meet the USA TODAY journalist because she's always excited to share the Cheekin story.

Jana enthusiastically greeted the reporter and pointed to a piece of artwork on the wall, launching into the artist's life story. "She grew up on a farm as one of eight children," Jana began, then illustrated the course of the artist's life in captivating detail, including her experiences with tornadoes, droughts, floods, and financial challenges. The reporter listened intently, interested in the founder's spirited storytelling while confused about how it related to the interview topic: the company vision.

Without taking a breath, Jana pivoted to a new topic: technology. She described how her prior experience at various tech companies helps her understand how to prioritize and streamline processes.

"And then the data!" she exclaimed. "The data is rich and so important. It provides a window into safety, customer demand, cost/

benefit analysis, and keyholes into new products." As Jana described all of this in rapid fire, her public relations rep jumped in. "Jana, should we visit the lab to demonstrate how innovation ties into your vision?"

"Oh yes, the lab!" Jana responded. "Our research scientists are *brilliant*. Their focus on perfecting current products, and their curiosity about developing new ones, is unmatched!"

The reporter then interrupted Jana with a question about new products. Jana nodded and rattled off a series of non sequiturs that loosely formed a tapestry of ideas around the environment, farming practices, and consumers' evolving preferences. While interesting, her response did not answer the reporter's question.

Over the course of 45 minutes, Jana had skimmed over various topics ranging from technology to data to food products, with seemingly non-related economic and social issues sprinkled in. At the end, the reporter was both impressed and bewildered. Jana's homily was barely over when she was pulled into a meeting with her investors. She enthusiastically waved goodbye to the reporter.

"Wow, she's . . . zealous," the reporter said, "but I'm not sure I understand the significance of the artwork."

"Yes," the public relations rep agreed. "Jana is passionate about a broad range of topics. She sprints rather than speaks."

Jana's interest in a wide smattering of topics comes at a cost. Rather than revealing her brilliance, her pivots can be regarded as scattered. When the article was published, it focused on the eccentric founder's ebullience rather than on her business savvy or Cheekin's vision.

::

Jana's passion would have been better followed, retained, and retold by the reporter if she had scaffolded her exuberance with structure. If she had developed and communicated three clear messages, the USA TODAY piece would have reflected a clear explanation of Cheekin's vision.

Perhaps you, too, have experienced messy content. Have you ever been to a rehearsal dinner where a guest, usually a friend of the groom, stands up and delivers a deplorable speech? There are many reasons for hideous speeches including inappropriate stories (*Hello, not prioritizing listeners*), too much booze (*it's free, why not?*), and a rambling mess of information (*no structure or forethought*).

You don't have to attend a rehearsal dinner to suffer through a chaotic speech. Think about your Uncle Mike's Thanksgiving trip down memory lane, or presidential updates about COVID-19, not to mention way too many work updates that amble along with no clear point.

You've likely attended meetings where you had no idea what the speaker was saying. You know, the one where the presenter dives in the weeds, explaining the attributes of a solution to a problem you didn't even know you had.

It's happened to each and every one of us.

How Does Your Audience Benefit From Structure?

Unfortunately, speakers have a "curse of knowledge:" a presumption that their listeners have the background or context to understand what they're hearing. Believe it or not, you too have this curse. You know your material so well that, at times, you may forget that others need to orient themselves to what you are sharing. Creating structure (and delivering concrete language) for your listeners is particularly important when they hear information for the first time.

As a speaker, it's crucial to overcome your curse of knowledge and grapple with your listeners' attention spans. Would you believe that science-backed brain activity shows a listener's attention span is as short as eight seconds long. To put that in perspective, the attention span of a goldfish is nine seconds long.[21] So, as you communicate, be mindful that your listeners may be more distracted than the inhabitants of the fish tank in your dentist's waiting room!

Organizing your content helps listeners because they can:

21 McSpadden, Kevin. "You Now Have a Shorter Attention Span Than a Goldfish." *Time*, 14 May 2015.

1. Track your subject matter

Structure categorizes and contextualizes your content to help an audience track what you are saying. Remember, your listeners are spacing out every eight seconds, and potentially more often as they multitask in a virtual environment, so structure serves as a map to let them know where the conversation is headed, and when to pay close attention to the highlights.

2. Retain and share

Framework acts like educational scaffolding, allowing your listeners to both retain and share your information. When you separate content into distinct parts, your listeners can more easily remember it. Retaining information is challenging when listening to a dense monologue.

3. Prevent distractions

Structure prevents the ol' *listener-focused-on-their-question* problem. We've all been in the situation where we hear a speaker say something that prompts a question in our head. When you share structured information at the *start* of your communication, listeners will more readily tune in because they know what's coming.

"The brain can't process everything in the environment. It's developed those filtering processes that allow it to focus on some information at the expense of other information."[22] So, remember: rather than let your listener try to determine the upshot, provide structure for your ideas so they can grasp the most important information.

How Does Structure Benefit You?

Now that we've established how structure helps your listeners, let's shift to how organizing your content will help *you*. Speakers benefit from structure because they can:

---

22 Cepelewicz, Jordana. "To Pay Attention, the Brain Uses Filters, Not a Spotlight." *Quanta Magazine*, 24 Sept. 2019.

1. **Remember more information**

Grouping items together makes it easier to remember more content. In fact, psychologists have a name for this phenomenon, and it's called "chunking." We can test this concept by looking at a ten-digit number. If I told you to look at these numbers and memorize them in order—9173211209—you might feel stressed doing so. If, instead, I divided them into three parts (917) 321-1209, like a phone number, it would be easier to remember.

2. **Elevate the important stuff**

When you create content that has framework, it's organized into a simple but powerful outline, which is key to remembering and communicating your essential ideas.

3. **Communicate authentically**

Categorizing your content makes it easy to focus on the outline; this means you don't need to worry about all the details. You can utilize your freed-up mental space to concentrate on what's really important: making a connection with your listener.

How to Structure

Dating back to the days of Plato, the gold standard of speaking is to structure content into threes. Examples of this, the power of threes, are everywhere. The 1776 Declaration of Independence lists three inalienable rights: life, liberty, and the pursuit of happiness. Public service announcements use threes: from stop, drop, and roll (fire prevention) to Australia's Slip Slop Slap campaign to promote sun protection (slip on a shirt, slop on sunscreen, slap on a hat). Since our brains are attuned, socialized, and accustomed (see what I did there?) to remembering items categorized into threes, it makes sense to use this structure when we're speaking up.

Categories of three can follow a linear approach like Phase 1, Phase 2, Phase 3. They can also delineate different lines of business as in product, marketing, and sales.

Other examples of this include:

- Problem, Solution, Next Steps
- What, Why, How (example: specific project, why it's important, how we'll implement it)
- Solution, Alternative, Costs
- Projection, Reality, Difference

Believe it or not, the actual categories you select are not as important as simply structuring your content, so don't overthink it.

The Speak Up Structure tool provides a straightforward but powerful framework that helps you categorize your overarching topic into three components. For example, if your topic is diversity, your three categories might be: current company composition, diversity goals, and next steps.

Communicate Using Your Speak Up Structure Tool

1. Briefly name your topic at the start of your communication. For example, "Today's topic is diversity."
2. Next, share a short agenda stating each category's name. For example, "We'll discuss our current company composition

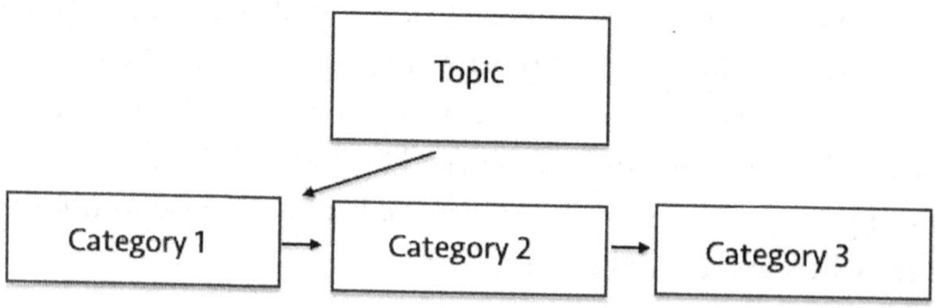

An example using the diversity topic:

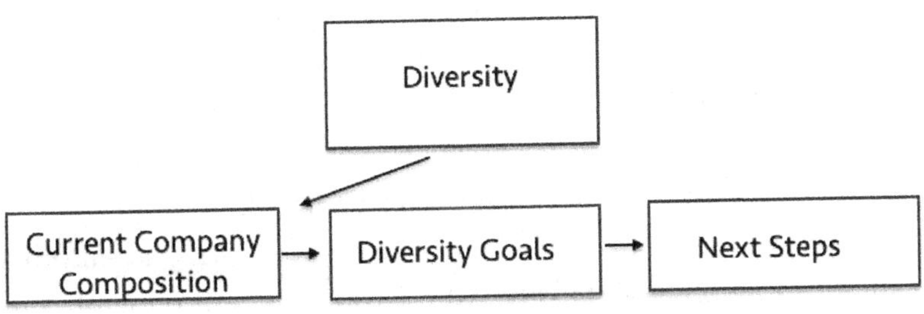

In identifying the topic and categories up front, you've prepared your listener for what they can expect.

Next up? Sharing more details about each category.

CLIENT PERSPECTIVE

Katja worried about her upcoming board presentation. The last time she presented to the board, she felt scattered and all over the place despite—or because of—hours spent preparing.

She contacted me for coaching and I introduced her to the Speak Up Structure Tool. She was amazed that something so simple could transform her thoughts into neat packets of information.

After the meeting she sent a note saying, "Wow! The structure tool was transformative. I felt confident entering the meeting and, guess what? I nailed my presentation!"

Stick to Three

You may be tempted to include more than three categories of information. Clients tell me, "My audience is very smart. They can handle more than that." You're right; your audience **is** smart, and they may be able to digest more than three categories, but why create a cognitive burden on them? We are already distracted by so much daily input—make listening great again.

Michael Scott, played by actor Steve Carell on the long-running TV sitcom *The Office*, is potentially the worst leader and communicator of all time (but arguably one of the most hilarious characters). When asked to impart information to a graduate school class, Michael would have done well to follow a structure of threes. "There are four kinds of business," he said. "Tourism. Food service. Railroad, and sales. And hospitals slash manufacturing. And air travel."

If you were attending Michael's class, and actually attempting to retain information, you'd likely exit the room and not remember more than one or two things he said. If, instead, Michael opened up by saying, "There are three categories of business: Hospitality, Transportation, and Health," then followed up with descriptions and examples of each, you would be more apt to track and take in the information.

Impromptu Speaking

One of the most common reasons clients approach me is they don't know how to contribute to meetings. Again, having a structure of three helps with this.

Wait, what? *Planned impromptu speaking?* Isn't that an oxymoron? While it's true that impromptu is defined as "composed or uttered without previous preparation," you *can* prepare to contribute during meetings and at work.[23]

Here's how. First, anticipate that you'll be called on at every meeting you attend. If you go into a meeting with that mindset, you'll be mentally prepared to contribute and more likely to identify one, two, or three key messages that are relevant. Your messages can reflect your unique understanding about the topic, your opinions about said topic, or a combination of both.

For example, to prepare for a meeting about a marketing roadshow, you might compose the following messages:

1. We should focus on hands-on demonstrations.
2. Our users are mostly located in coastal cities.
3. The marketing materials are currently too wordy.

---

23 "impromtu." *Merriam-Webster.com*. Merriam-Webster, 2011.

By crafting messages before your meeting, you'll be prepared to share information when the opportunity strikes.

On a personal note, when I started sharing videos on social media, I felt comfortable because I had structured my content and rehearsed before recording. On the other hand, when I was a guest on a podcast, I wasn't given the questions in advance, which made me uneasy. To prepare, I identified three key messages I wanted to share plus an example to illustrate each one. With those messages crafted and rehearsed, I could comfortably answer each question sent my way.

> **"If you invest the time earlier to create structure and process around communication, planning, and goal-setting, you can prevent missteps before they occur."**
>
> CHRISTINE TSAI, CEO and founding partner of 500 startups

EXERCISES

Exercise 1: Biography Exercise

What: Record your biography.

Why: Because of our rich and varied personal experiences, speaking about ourselves is typically more difficult than it seems.

How:

1. Use the voice recording feature on your phone to record your life story or your "biography." You can start when you were a kid, or when you were in college, or with your first job. You can focus on your personal story, your professional story, or a combination of both. Include as many details as you would like because this is an exercise for you, and only you. In other words, feel free to share as much information as you would like without worrying about how it'll be perceived by others. The only requirement is you must talk for at least one minute.
2. Listen to your recording. Focus on your content rather than on the sound of your voice. What did you notice? Would you change any information or how you structured your content if you had the opportunity to do so? Good news: in Exercise 2 you have the opportunity to restructure your content and make another recording.

....

Exercise 2: Organize Your Biography

What: Organize your biography by adding structure.

Why: Structure makes content delivery easier for you to communicate, and straightforward for your audience to digest.

How:

1. Organize your life story into three parts such as:

- Chronological (your schooling years, first job, and current career)

- Your interests (soccer, travel, and research),
- Your relationships (siblings, roommates, romantic)

  OR
- Structured into any three parts you would like to use.

  Don't overthink it. The important instruction is to divide your life experiences into three categories.

2. Re-record your biography using the three parts you just identified. Again, be sure to speak for at least one minute.
3. Listen to your recording then answer the following questions:

   What did you notice?

   How does "Take 1" compare to "Take 2"?

   If you were to create a third "Take," would you structure your content the same way? The beauty about structure is there is no right or wrong way to do it. Any three-part structure is better than a "data dump" of information.

Exercise 3: Prepare to Be Spontaneous

What: Create a practice that helps you prepare to speak up during meetings.

Why: Many of us fear these moments, yet we know we need to contribute. Planning helps you feel prepared.

How: *Before the meeting*

1. Look at your calendar to see what meetings you have during the next week or month. Identify one where you know it's important for you to contribute.
2. Assess the situation. Who will be in the room and what do they need to know? Next, what is the business context?

3. Craft three key messages that meet your listeners' needs and are relevant to the business context.
4. Practice saying each message out loud.

During the meeting

Listen for openings during the meeting where you can add value by speaking one of your key messages.

Pro Tip: Add supporting documentation like a statistic, story, or client example to bring your key messages to life.

As an example, if a meeting is focused on creating a more diverse employee pipeline, come to the table armed with statistics about the demographics of recruiting events your company currently attends.

Alternatively, research how another company approached the problem, e.g., "eBay increased their diverse applicant pipeline by . . . "

CHAPTER 9

Persuade

Nia is the ambitious first-time CEO of a cutting-edge tech company. On a recent call with potential investors, she described her company as she always does, starting with where she studied, where she met the founder, and a rambling list of her accomplishments.

Fourteen minutes into the pitch, Nia began to explain the big problem her start-up is looking to solve: they plan to change the way people view nutrition and exercise. Obesity is an epidemic, and a $12 billion problem. Investors were interested, however, their interest was tempered by the knowledge that countless other companies and health initiatives have tried to address this same problem in vain. They weren't optimistic that Nia had identified the answer.

Finally, at minute 18 she said, "We partnered with Stanford to test our gaming app. Initial results show our app creates behavior change."

Whhaaa??? It took her 18 minutes to get to the most *important nugget:* "Our app works! We know how to create behavior change and solve a $12 billion problem."

::

And this, my reader, is what should have been the lead. By minute five the investors need to know this crucial information: "We created an app that generates changes in nutrition and exercise habits."

The remaining time can be spent explaining how the app works and answering investors' likely questions.

In case you don't know the venture capitalist or funding world, think about the busiest person you know. This person is busy not only on paper but also in their mind. They may also be the *least* patient person you will ever encounter. Do you think this person wants to hear the details of Nia's long, winding road to her position as CEO, or to the details about how the app was created? No. They need the bottom line: "*We have a solution to one of the largest and most lucrative problems to face modern society.*" *That* is what gets their attention.

Nia made a common and fatal flaw: TMI. She shared too much information, and in this situation, both the quantity and quality of information mattered. More is not always more. You don't want to overwhelm your listeners with information and, as we discussed in the last chapter, it's imperative you share content that will firmly hold their attention.

Data Overload — And Why It's Important to Not Do It

Every day, your listeners are bombarded by email, texts, and Slack messages, not to mention constant imagery, videos, and ads on websites and social media. They are inundated with information, so when listeners enter a meeting, likely distracted by their to-do lists and meeting goals, they unfortunately may not be "all ears." (Remember, your listeners' attention span can be as short as eight seconds.)

Speakers, on the other hand, often make the mistake of deciding, "I'll tell my listener everything, then they can pick and choose which parts are relevant." It's important to realize this universal truth: your listeners need the bottom line! If you give them too much information, external and internal distractions drown out your communication and your listeners tune out. And the busier she is, the more she needs to hear the most pertinent information. You need to cut through the noise, fight through the distractions, and capture their attention.

Persuasion Strategy 1: Create the Bottom Line

So, how do you create a bottom line? That may seem like a silly question with a simple answer, but it's actually surprisingly hard to pare down our content. Why? Because we love our content. We conceived it, we produced it, and we want to protect it. The process of deciding the most important part feels a little bit like choosing a favorite puppy from a litter of ten.

To start that difficult process, first remove the background and extraneous detail. Apply the motto coined by Procter & Gamble's former CEO: "keep it *Sesame Street* simple."[24] This, too, is easier said than done. As speakers, we want to share the backstory, the process detailing how we arrived at a conclusion. And yet what worked for us in crafting school essays is not what works in the boardroom!

Many companies have their own name for the "Sesame Street Simple" concept. For some, it's the BLUF, or Bottom Line up Front. For others, it's the BLOT, or Bottom Line on Top. Consulting companies, like Deloitte or McKinsey & Company, subscribe to the Pyramid Principle. Regardless of the formula name, almost all my clients struggle to start with the headline.

At a recent team meeting, Celia shared her recommendation to work with a design firm we'll call ABC:

::

"Six weeks ago, we agreed we needed to redo our website to showcase our new product offerings. With that in mind, I collected names of reputable web design companies by asking my marketing network. I reached out to four recommended firms to understand their process, see their prior work, and obtain a quote. One of the firms was inundated with work and unable to start our project for three months. Another firm did not have enough relevant client examples to share. That left us with ABC and XYZ web design firms. Both have beautiful

24 Sutton, Robert I. "Why Bosses Ought to Be More Interested in What Is True Than What Is New." *Fast Company*, 10 Aug. 2010.

client examples that reflect the look and feel we want to create. Both are available to start within two weeks and both have people who understand our goals. I asked for bids and XYZ's bid came back 20% higher than ABC's. Since all other factors are the same, I recommend contracting with ABC firm."

::

Here's what Celia should have said: "We should contract with ABC firm because they have relevant experience and their bid aligned with our budget, which is 20% less than the second bid."

See the difference? The first conversation was 10 sentences long compared to the second version's single sentence. I've listened to countless audio recordings of conversations and can confirm that version one is actually streamlined compared to those that contain even more extraneous details like, "It took me a while to connect with XYZ firm because their lead designer was on vacation. Then we were out of the office on our team retreat, but we eventually connected, and their team is really competent."

Nobody cares.

To distill your content into a "headline," or single statement, answer the questions in the last chapter including, "What does my audience **really** care about?" "What do they need to hear?" or "What's in it for them?" In Nia's case, the WIIFMs for her investor audience are business viability and investment returns. Simply put, they want to make money. With this in mind, her headline should read, "My company created an app that is proven to create behavior change in the obese population, which is a $12 billion market."

Your listeners' immediate concerns must be addressed before they are ready to hear how the solution works, who will be running the company, or an outline of the next steps.

Sharing the bottom line requires restraint. It might feel strange but, with practice, it becomes second nature. If you're worried that your listeners won't get what they need with a headline, fear not. Share the essence, pause, then observe how your listener reacts. At this point, your listener may ask questions. Or by gauging the looks on their faces, you can determine if they want to hear more, and add details. The best outcome? It's clear they're on board with your headline, so you end early, giving everyone the gift of time.

Persuasion Strategy 2: Make It about Them

There are two parts to this persuasion strategy:

1. Include benefits

To create interest and buy-in, your listener needs to know how your headline impacts them. The best way to do this is to incorporate a benefit i.e., the impact on your listener, directly after your bottom-line statement.

For example, if your headline is, "We should invest in a new website," your recommendation alone may not land with your listener. They will pay more attention when you add a benefit or an impact that is relevant to them. Let's say you're speaking to the finance department, so your recommendation and benefit might sound like, "We should invest in a new website that streamlines the purchase process and yields more revenue." By nature of immediate gratification, that should fire up the finance team, no?

Okay, but now you are pivoting, and speaking to the human resources department, so you will adapt the statement to their needs, which include focusing on employee benefits. Your headline might be, "We should invest in a new website so employees can access information about their medical and retirement plans in one location."

In other words, add a benefit or impact that is relevant to your audience or answers the WIIFM. How do you know what's in it for them? Exercise 4 will help you determine your audience's values and motivations.

A common mistake speakers make when trying to be persuasive is assuming the listener shares your values. For example, as a speaker, I may value a thorough process, but my listener values efficiency. If I say, "We should implement these new steps and standardize the process so we can create the most accurate measurements," the listener may get annoyed at the idea of adding more steps because he just wants it done. Now.

It takes discipline to think about your listeners' values *and* to craft information relevant to them, but it's worth the effort. Imagine how much more successful Nia would have been had she thought about her audience before spending 18 minutes waxing on about the company history and her credentials.

2. Replace "I" statements

Have you ever noticed how often you—and people around you—start sentences with the words "I" or "my"? If you pay attention you will hear, "I think," or "My idea is," over and over.

What's wrong with an "I" or a "my"? On the surface, they're innocuous, personable words. The problem is your listener hears those words and subconsciously thinks, "This is an idea about *them*" or "This won't be relevant to me."

The other problem with "I" statements is they sound like favors. "I think we should consider this strategy" can be interpreted as, "Would you consider this strategy as a favor to me?" *Convert your favors into facts.*

There are two ways to do this. First, use "we" and "our," which are inclusive words, to replace "I" and "my."

Examples include:

Original Version:	**Revised Version:**
"I think we should consider the risks."	"We should consider the risks."
"My priority is to solve the quality control problem."	"Our priority is solving the quality control problem."

The second way to replace "I" statements is to make the sentences assertive by removing personal pronouns. This method involves replacing, "I," "my," "we" and "our" with the pronoun "it" as in "It's important" or "It's critical," or removing pronouns altogether to make declarative statements like, "The priority is" or "The first step is."

Examples include:

"I think it is important to . . . "	"It is critical to . . . "
"My priority is . . .	"The priority is . . . "
"We should think about safety."	"Safety needs to be top of mind."

Persuasion Strategy 3: Create Context

When people communicate at work, they often make big statements like, "It will cost $240,000," or "We will save two million dollars," or "The new process takes five weeks to complete." But what do these statements really mean? In order for large numbers to land, you need to contextualize the data for your listener.

You can create relevance by adding information that places the number in context for your listener. The statement, "It will cost $240,000," takes on a completely different meaning if the remaining information is, "and the budget for this project is only $100,000," versus the extra information, "and it will generate $1.2 million in additional revenue."

Persuasion Strategy 4: Crisp Content

A fourth way to be persuasive is to communicate in a clear, assertive manner. This includes avoiding apologies, self-deprecation, and dismissive language. Why? It dilutes your content.

Below is a chart of statements you may say at work, and an example of how to make those statements more crisp and assertive.

What We Often Say:	What is More Persuasive:
I haven't given this much thought	One idea is to . . .
I haven't completed the analysis	We should examine . . .
I'm no expert	One recommendation is . . .
I might be wrong	Let's consider . . .
Maybe we should . . . I sort of wonder if . . . We should review the plan, don't you think? Perhaps we should look at the numbers? I think maybe we should consider the alternatives	We should . . . We need to . . . Let's It's important to . . . It's critical (or imperative) to . . .
I'm sorry to bother you	Should we discuss this now or later?
I tend to agree	That is absolutely right, and here's why
This will just take a minute	Here are the highlights from the meeting
What if we thought about . . .	A good option is . . .

Checklist for Planning Persuasive Communication

1. Create a headline by removing the background information and extraneous detail.
2. Identify the benefit or the impact of your headline on your listeners.
3. Replace "I" statements with inclusive language ("we / our") or with declarative statements ("It is important to . . . ")
4. Use crisp content (avoid disclaimers, apologies, etc.).

EXERCISES

Exercise 1: Problem / Solution Brainstorm

What: Identify a list of problems and solutions related to an aspect of your job.

Why: Brainstorms produce some of our best ideas.

How:
1. Using the voice memo feature on your phone, record yourself explaining:
   - All the problems or challenges you face in your current role (or that your company faces).
   - Any and all solutions you have for making your job or the company more effective.
2. Speak as long as you like and include as many details as you like.

You may be tempted to overthink or wonder how to do this exercise the "right" way. Rest assured: *there is no right way!* The key is to share every idea you have without editing yourself.

Here are three reasons why we want to communicate in this "raw" form:

1. Sometimes our best ideas emerge from a top-of-mind rambling. When you attempt to edit or refine from the start, you might lose some golden nuggets.

2. You can determine if your natural brainstorming sounds murky or convoluted to your listener. You may feel like you're rambling, but find that your content actually made perfect sense. Or you realize that you were indeed rambling, so you recognize the benefit of iterating and rehearsing before speaking opportunities.
3. This process builds our rehearsal muscle, which is useful to flex before any Speak Up opportunity.

Exercise 2: Brainstorm — Listen

What: Listen to your own ideas.

Why: How you feel when you communicate is always different from what other people observe. By listening, you'll have a better sense of how clearly you communicate and how persuasive your solutions tend to be.

How:

1. Listen closely, focusing on the *content* you shared, not on the sound or characteristics of your voice. (This is hard! After this exercise, you can return to Chapters 1, 3, or 4 to review how to finesse specific characteristics of your voice.)
2. Answer the questions below in your Speak Up journal:
    - What content did you include at the start of your communication?
    - Did you include any extraneous information your listener does not need or want to hear?
    - What information did you include that feels very important or very relevant to share with your listener?
    - When did you propose solutions or ideas your listener will care about?

Based on what you heard, write your headline (or bottom line) of your recording.

As a reminder, the headline that Celia should have shared is:

"We should contract with ABC because they have relevant experience and their bid aligned with our budget, which is 20% less than the second bid."

Write your bottom line in your Speak Up journal.

Exercise 3: Headline Hunter

What: Use Persuasion Strategy #1 to communicate the Bottom Line on Top.

Why: Starting with the bottom line is not always intuitive. This method requires restraint and practice.

How:

1. Re-record the content you shared in Exercise 1. This time, start with the headline, then describe the challenges or details.
2. Listen to the audio recording and answer the following questions:
   - Which version would resonate better with someone who is very busy?
   - Which version would appeal to an analytical, process-oriented listener?
   - How can you appeal to both types of listeners?

Exercise 4: Add Benefits

What: Add benefits to your headline.

Why: Your audience needs to hear—early on—how your information will impact them.

How:
1. Identify your audience's values and motivations by answering the following questions in your journal.
   - What do your listeners care most about?
   - What gets them out of bed in the morning?
   - What worries them? What keeps them up at night?
   - What are their "rational" motivators? These are the incentives they are not afraid to share with others. For example, your listeners might tell you they're motivated by saving time, making money, innovating, or meeting customers' needs.
   - What are their "emotional" motivators? These are the values your listeners are less likely to share and may include fear, ego, looking good, receiving praise, resistance to change, keeping the peace, wanting to sound like the smartest person in the room, and so on.
2. State the headline, then immediately include a benefit (or impact) to your listener. For example, "It is important to determine the number of people we intend to hire next year," the headline, "so we can budget the amount we need for salaries and benefits," the benefit to your finance-focused audience.

Exercise 5: Refine Your Recommendation

What: Refine your recommendation by using Persuasive Strategy #2: Make it about Them.

Why: Because we communicate from the first person, we often include "I" or "my" statements. These are less persuasive than audience-focused language.

How:

1. Listen to your audio recordings again. Did you hear any "I" or "my" statements? If so, rewrite those statements by either:
2. Using inclusive language like "we" or "our" or replace personal pronouns with declarative statements ("It is critical to" or "The first priority is").

Exercise 6: Create Crisp Content

What: Use Persuasion Strategy #4: Crisp Content to refine your speaking style.

Why: When we add words or phrases such as "you know," "just," "kind of," it can weaken your idea and your credibility.

How:

1. Record a one-on-one meeting with important internal people on Zoom. Use Otter or another transcription program to read the dialogue. If you cannot transcribe your recording, listen to it instead.
2. Read the transcript looking for:
   - Qualifying statements or apologies
   - Statements that sound like questions
   - Words that weaken your ideas including "sort of," "maybe," etc.
3. Re-record your statements on your phone without apologies, disclaimers, or unnecessary filler words.

CHAPTER 10

Self-Talk

Sara is a brilliant but timid policy analyst who reached out to me with an important goal: she wanted to feel more confident in meetings. As we spoke, I learned she had been in the role for six years and felt underappreciated. Sara mostly enjoyed her data-rich job with the exception of one glaring element. "They want me to present in meetings to groups of more than 20 people. I hate that!" she complained. "I'd much rather upload my report and have them read it."

When I asked what was most difficult about presenting, Sara replied, "All of it." After a pause, she continued, "I guess, especially the idea that they'll ask questions. I just don't want to be put on the spot. I know I'll say the wrong thing. How could I not? The people in the room don't understand policy, but they think they do. And then, there are people who know—or think they know—the data better than I do. So, I just can't win."

Sara approached each meeting this way, dreading having to present and answer questions "knowing" she might provide the wrong answers. Her insecurity manifested itself in cold, clammy hands, a nauseated feeling, and a headache that lasted hours before and throughout each meeting.

Every time she entered the conference room for a meeting, she either stared at printouts laid on the table in front of her or buried her nose in her laptop. She did everything she could to avoid the gaze of those seated around the table. Sara never contributed ideas nor answered questions unless directly asked, and even then, she answered as quickly and curtly as possible.

This pattern repeated throughout her career. Each year, when her manager held her performance review, Sara was disappointed that despite having "met expectations" for her overall responsibilities, she never received an "exceeds expectations," nor was there a clear path for career progression. As a result, Sara's self-limiting beliefs (and, therefore, her behavior) adversely impacted her career.

During our first session, Sara and I catalogued her self-talk. Her three refrains were:

- "I say the wrong thing."
- "The people in the room understand the data better than I do."
- "I give the wrong answers."

Together, we examined each statement. Through a series of questions, we determined that Sara's beliefs were not absolute truths. We crafted new affirmations she could practice with evidence to support them. We identified a plan for how she could implement the reframed beliefs into her life, then we captured the ways in which Sara's personal and professional life would improve once she internalized these new assertions.

After three months of practicing this upgrade to her inner dialogue, Sara noticed a difference in her work. She no longer felt destined to fail when she entered policy meetings. Although they were still nerve-wracking, Sara found she enjoyed answering some of the questions that came her way. While Sara's was not an overnight turnaround story, she felt more confident and made noticeable improvements in her communication.

::

Like many of us, Sara's self-talk gets the best of her. Specifically, she:

- Overgeneralizes: she reaches a conclusion based on a single experience

- Catastrophizes: she expects the worst
- Filters out her positive contributions and instead focuses on the mistakes
- Fears she'll say the wrong thing, even though she has deep knowledge of the topic

Once she became aware of these habits, Sara was able to reverse her defeatist language and rewire her thoughts.

::

Isabelle is another client who overgeneralizes, catastrophizes, and filters her thinking. During a recent team meeting she shared the wrong date on a project timeline. She was only off by one calendar day, which was not material to the discussion, but she felt mortified when her colleague corrected her. Just then she heard mumbling around the room and thought, "Oh my god, they're snickering about me for so many reasons. They're laughing at me because I said the wrong date. I shouldn't have said that. I thought it was right. And I was so confident—but I was wrong. And I'm wearing the wrong thing. Everything I think I know and do must be wrong." The voice of her inner critic made the situation much bigger than the reality of making an inconsequential mistake.

::

You, too, have likely gone to the dark place where you think the worst of yourself after making a small mistake.

To improve on this, first, determine if you talk to yourself. When I ask that question during a training, about half of the room raises their hands. The other half become introspective. They appear to ask themselves, "Do I talk to myself? Hmm . . . Maybe? I guess I do when . . . "

The reality is we all do. It's true! *We talk to ourselves.* While it's hard to confirm the exact number of words people think per minute, experts estimate the number is between 500 and 4,000.[25] To put that in perspective, a fast talker speaks 150 words per minute. This means you think more than three words for every word you speak. And, for many of us, those extra thoughts are not helpful, particularly in stressful situations.

Before you share your ideas with the world, let's figure out what you're saying to yourself to make sure your self-talk serves you.

To evaluate how beneficial or detrimental your self-talk is, play the role of an anthropologist and catalogue your inner conversations. When you enter a nerve-wracking situation, make a mistake, or do something for the first time, try to notice your internal voice. You may not be aware how frequently self-critical thoughts pop into your head until you stop to notice them.

Strategies for Shifting Your Self-Talk

After taking inventory of the conversations that play out in your brain, you may realize your inner critic is taking up too much real estate. So, now what? Here are three strategies to shift your thinking from defeatist to resourceful.

1. Flip your script

Your script is the "story" you tell yourself. This is also known as self-limiting beliefs, or negative self-talk. This type of narrative is pervasive, and not just for women new in their careers. Your inner critic tends to rear its head more often when you try something new or when you are an "only" in the room.

Sara and I worked together to flip her script. First, she identified her most frequent self-critical thoughts. Next, she applied a version of Byron Katie's *The Work* to turn her self-talk around. We did this by closely examining Sara's own statement: *The people in the room understand the data better than I do.* Then she asked herself two questions.

25 Beck, Julie. "The Running Conversation in Your Head." *The Atlantic*, 23 Nov. 2016.

- "Is it true that people in the room understand the data better than me?"
  (And then, reallllly getting to the root of it . . .)
- "Is it *absolutely* true?"

When she realized that her fear was an overgeneralization, she agreed to flip her script to, "My data analysis is important to the people in the room."

After doing this work, Sara regularly monitored her mind-chatter, completed new turnaround stories and, over time, was able to rewire her thinking.

Now let's look at that same exercise for Isabelle, who worried about people in the room judging her. She would benefit by flipping "Everyone is judging me" to "The people in the room support me." Some other flips might be: "The audience wants to learn" or "The listeners are more focused on themselves than on me."

More examples of reframes include:

Self-Critical Thought	Flipped Script
I'm not a good presenter.	I engage listeners.
I hate speaking up at big meetings.	I am passionate about improving our processes.
I'm not qualified to speak about this topic.	I have useful information, or a unique or fresh perspective to share about this topic.
I could share my ideas, but nothing will change.	Imagine what is possible if I share my ideas?

Once you create your flipped script, repeat it like a mantra. Exercise 6 provides an opportunity for you to flip your script.

2. Dive in

It has long been thought that in order to change your mindset, you must change your behavior. While this does work, shifting your self-talk can be challenging!

In fact, it's possible that you are waiting for the right moment to feel confident or motivated before speaking up. The problem? Your self-talk keeps warning, "It's not safe. They might laugh at you." But this is your brain protecting you (as it did during the Stone Age) from being eaten by a saber-toothed tiger. While you no longer need saving from large predators, your brain is lazy and doesn't naturally update long-standing beliefs. If you wait for your brain to signal to your body, "I'm ready!" you will be waiting a very long time.

So, while it feels scary, when you "activate" (or lean into) your fears, you actually change your brain state. Better yet, the more you activate, the more positive these experiences will be. In other words, as Herminia Ibarra says in *Act Like a Leader, Think Like a Leader*, we need to adopt the behaviors of our aspirational selves to help us feel like our best selves.

Some liken this to "fake it 'til you make it," though I prefer to think of it as intentionally choosing bold behaviors. You gotta "do confident" to feel confident. So, be like Bronwyn: channel your inner rockstar.

3. (Re)move the target

A third challenge people face is obsessing about the outcome. You may wonder, "How will my recommendation land? Will the listeners approve or reject my idea? What if they think my suggestion is stupid? What if they agree to the idea but never implement it?"

Okay, stop. This focus on the outcome—the target—is a form of hiding. In *Playing Big*, Tara Mohr discusses how hiding can keep us feeling small and also prevents us from sharing our ideas with the world.

Rather than expending energy on the outcome, which you cannot control, you'll feel more resourceful if you move (or remove) the target and focus on the process instead.

Here's a real-world example. I became overly focused on the target while writing this book. First, I spent time worrying that no one would read it. Then, I spent too much time consumed with how people would react to it. I became paralyzed worrying about an outcome I could not control. So I removed the target and redefined what, for me, would feel like success: enjoying the process of creating something I know will be useful for the world.

Only then could I let go of the doubt that plagued my creative process.

Help — It's Not Working!

Now that you are noticing and reframing the way you speak to yourself, you may feel the new stories just don't stick. Don't worry. This is normal. Changing your inner dialogue is hard. If you define your mindset as a habitual way of thinking, then you have developed these habits over many years. So, it can't shift overnight. Your brain relies on the self-limiting beliefs that it's become stuck on, sometimes for years. You can envision this by thinking of your self-talk like a well-worn sled track. When you position a sled at the crest of a snowy hill, it wants to veer toward the path of least resistance—the one that is well-worn and easy to glide down. It takes deliberate attention and practice to create a new route, but it's worth the effort. Why? Because your brain is taking notes.

"What most of us think of as fear is primarily a mental process of imagining situations that do not exist in the moment."

CHERI HUBER, Zen Teacher

EXERCISES

Exercise 1: Channel Joy

What: Identify a time when you felt on top of the world.

Why: Reflecting on a time when you felt joyful and confident can help you channel those feelings when self-doubt creeps in.

How:

1. Identify a time when you felt confident and on top of your game. This could be an event that happened anytime during your life.

   An example is the afternoon you spent hours on the swing after school. You remember pumping your legs so hard, and soaring high into the sky. Then, when you hit the peak point, you jumped and flew through the air feeling weightless and free.

2. Close your eyes and remember your moment of pure joy.
3. Write down the following:
   - Your self-talk during this joyful time. If you don't recall, write down what you imagine it would be.
   - Your mood, the emotions felt, any behaviors you noticed. Label each one. (For example: enthusiasm, which felt like buzzing in my chest.)
   - How you felt during the event, as well as after.

Exercise 2: The Name Exercise

What: A new activity that provides insight into your self-talk.

Why: Our thoughts are built on decades of experience. It's useful to know what patterns of self-talk emerge when we experience a new activity.

How:

1. Grab a piece of paper, a pen, and a timer. (Think watch, phone, microwave—any timer will do.)
2. For 30 seconds, write your name, however you like, as many times as you can. While you're writing, notice what you're thinking and feeling. Ready, Set, Go!
3. When you're finished, take a *deep breath*.
4. Identify what you were saying to yourself during the exercise. When I lead this activity during a workshop, participants share a range of thoughts including, "Am I doing this right?" "What is the point of this exercise?" "My handwriting sucks," "I don't know if I should write my full name or my nickname."

The instructions for this exercise are intentionally vague as it mimics a work situation where you don't know all the "rules" or the context and details. Your self-talk during this exercise is typically similar to what you tell yourself in ambiguous work situations.

If your thoughts were self-judging, ("Am I doing this right?" or "My handwriting sucks") or self-doubt ("I don't know if I should write my full name, or . . . "), you likely experience these types of thoughts when you communicate. In Exercise 4 you will learn how to reverse self-judging thoughts.

Exercise 3: Intimidating and Supportive Circles

What: An exercise to identify when you feel resourceful and when you do not.

Why: Identifying the situations and people who make you feel big or small will provide important insight.

How:

1. On a piece of paper draw an aerial view of a round table, i.e., looking down at the table. Surround your table with 4-6 circles that represent chairs. Within each circle write the name of a person who intimidates you or makes you feel apprehensive, nervous, or uncomfortable.
2. Imagine speaking to this group of people. What thoughts arise? What emotions do you notice? What types of behaviors will emerge when you speak to this group of people?
3. Draw a second table. This time, fill the seats with people—anyone in the world—who support you, encourage you, and with whom you feel most confident. You can get creative with this exercise and even list people you don't personally know.
4. When you imagine speaking to this group of people, what thoughts arise? What about moods? What behaviors will show up when you speak to these people?
5. Compare how you felt when you imagined presenting to intimidating people versus how you felt when you imagined presenting to supportive people.
   - How do your thoughts differ?
   - How do your behaviors differ?
   - How will your results differ?

You'll likely notice a clear difference between your reactions speaking to a supportive group versus one that feels intimidating. But is the difference in your reactions based on reality? The next exercise helps us determine how authentic our fears actually are.

Exercise 4: Walk the Tightrope

What: A physical exercise to see the power of your self-talk.

Why: Our fears are often irrational, but they *feel real.* This exercise contextualizes the fear of heights.

How:

1. Find a rope, measuring tape, or wooden board that is at least 18 inches long, and place it on the ground. This is your tightrope.
2. Walk along the top of the item and notice how easy or difficult it feels to do so.
3. Imagine your tightrope is three feet in the air. Now imagine walking on it. Would you be able to walk with the same confidence as you did when the rope, measuring tape or board was on the ground?
4. Finally, imagine you placed the object 20 feet in the air. Would you feel confident walking now?

The risks have increased: falling off a tightrope placed on the ground is not the same as falling from 20 feet in the air, but your ability to walk across it has not changed. What does change? Your self-talk and your mindset.

Think back to Exercise 3 about the two tables, one with intimidating people and one that feels supportive. Are you able to humanize the individuals in the nerve-inducing room? Can you recognize that each person in that room has good days and bad days? Can you find compassion for them by remembering that, just like you, each one of them needs to sleep and eat and use the restroom?

More importantly, your skills have not changed. You have the same capacity to speak confidently when you talk to supportive people as when you speak to intimidating people. In the next exercise you will explore how to get there.

Exercise 5: Write a Letter to Your Future Self

What: A goal-setting exercise.

Why: Envisioning the future makes it more likely you'll work towards it.

How:

1. 1. Pick a date between 5 and 50 years from now.
2. Think about who you will be at that time. Here are some prompts to get your creative juices flowing:
    - What is my life like?
    - What am I good at?
    - What am I proud of?
    - Where did I succeed?
    - Where did I fail?
    - What have I learned in the process?
    - How have I grown as a person?
3. Write a letter and include anything that comes to mind. This letter is just for you, so be as open and thorough as possible.
4. Seal the letter in an envelope and write the "open on" date on the envelope. Store your letter in a safe place.

Exercise 6: Flip Your Script

What: A framework for changing your critical thought (or your story) based on Byron Katie's introspective series of questions, *The Work.*

Why: We typically repeat the same limiting beliefs over and over. Flipping this script creates a new story to repeat and internalize.

How:

1. Identify the stories you tell yourself that don't serve you well. *For example: "I get tongue-tied when I speak to the CEO."*

   Write one of these stories in your journal.

2. Ask yourself: "Is my story true? Is it **absolutely** true?"

3. Flip your script: Change your story to the opposite point of view. Stretch to the place where you want to be, e.g., *"I get nervous when I present to the CEO" becomes "I feel confident whenever I present to the CEO."*

4. Identify three pieces of evidence that support your new script. Get specific and write them in your journal.

   Examples of evidence:
   - *When I spoke to the CEO last month, I was well prepared and made my points clearly.*
   - *Last week I talked easily to the CEO about her upcoming vacation.*
   - *During the team meeting, I discussed the data the CEO requested.*

5. Identify three actions you will take to support your new script.

   Examples of actions:
   - *I will focus on breathing to calm down when speaking to the CEO.*
   - *I will write out the three messages I want to say in advance of conversations with the CEO.*

   - *I will focus on my posture and body language during meetings with the CEO.*

6. Describe three ways your life and career will significantly improve with this new script.
7. Repeat your flipped script over and over. Notice how it feels in your head, your heart, and your body. Repeat the process until you feel your most empowered self.

CHAPTER 11

Nerves

Jessy was a hard worker who was frequently praised for her detailed analyses. She anticipated what information the team would want to know, and they were pleased with her results. This team meeting was no exception. All was going well until her boss dropped a bomb. "We'd like you to present your market analysis at the next board meeting." Jessy's competent posture evaporated. Her shoulders dropped a couple of inches as she shrank in the chair.

"No. Way!" Jessy screamed inside, "I cannot do it. I will not do it. Speak to the board of directors? My only interaction with them has been viewing their faces and bios on the company website, for God's sake! I don't know them. And they don't know me! This is a disaster."

Her nightmare was disrupted with, "Oh, and by the way, the board meeting is on March 6th. Two weeks to prep. Plenty of time. You've got this."

Jessy was paralyzed with fear. "What if I say something stupid? What if I stutter? What happens when the board realizes I'm not an expert? Who am I to present to this group of accomplished real estate experts?" Her head began to spin.

A week later, her supervisor checked on her progress. As he predicted, Jessy's preparation was on target. She had transformed volumes of data into pie charts and bar graphs shaded in the company's brand colors. The opportunities were clearly outlined, as were the risks, along with strategies for how to address each one.

Predictably, Jessy's manager was pleased with the progress and plans to distribute the materials to the board members that afternoon. Jessy felt the blood drain from her face.

Three days before the meeting, Jessy woke up in a cold sweat. Her head was pounding, her tongue felt thick, and she was short of breath. Her initial thought was, "Thank God I'm sick. My boss will have to present in my place." As she trudged out of bed into a warm shower, she recognized the symptoms for what they were: anxiety. "This is ridiculous," she thought. "Clearly I cannot present if the mere thought of speaking to the board gives me a panic attack. Maybe I can attend the meeting by phone."

But her dream of presenting by phone was shattered when she stumbled into the office at 9:07, a solid 37 minutes later than usual. Her boss approached her before she had a chance to set down her bag or remove her coat. "Great news! I've received notes from several board members. They are pleased as punch and cannot wait to meet you!"

"Shit!" Jessy screamed in her head, "I am on the hook."

Realizing her presentation would go on as planned, Jessy devised a new strategy: she'd take a shot of vodka 30 minutes before the meeting. "What kind would work best?" she wondered. She'd always been a Tito's fan, but the rosé vodkas might do the trick beautifully. Her boss walked by her desk, shaking her back to reality. She needed another strategy.

Near tears, Jessy called her college roommate, a public defender whose assertive style had protected many innocent clients. "Help! I don't know what I'm doing. I'm scared shitless."

Her friend coached her to breathe, relax, and hold off on the vodka until after the presentation. Then she asked a few questions. "How well do you know this topic?"

"Really well. These are my accounts and I've done all the analysis."

"What are the benefits of you presenting this information over your boss?"

With that question, Jessy realized she had earned the right to present to the board. Because the truth is, Jessy would never want her younger sister nor the newer associates to see her boss representing her hard work at an important meeting.

With her friend's help, Jessy reoriented her thinking away from potential fumbles and focused on how much she had to share, and what the board of directors would learn. Jessy also concentrated on how this experience would make her a role model for the younger associates. "What a bad-ass! I'm speaking to the frickin' board of directors!" Jessy told herself.

On the evening of the board meeting, Jessy abstained from the booze. She entered the room, convinced the board members could see the tremble in her hand. She tried to breathe through the nerves. Through the initial 20 minutes of updates and financials, Jessy sat tall, and silently repeated her mantra, "I know my stuff. The board wants to hear this information."

When it was her turn to speak, Jessy took a deep breath and began, "The health care sector analytics are compelling. We've beaten our predictions in the St. Louis, Kansas City, Tallahassee, and Nashville markets by an average of 18%. On the other hand, we're 7% below the predicted model in the mid-Atlantic market. Here's the plan for how to address the miss."

She detailed the market data she knew like the back of her hand. The board asked clarifying questions about next steps. Then the head of the board leaned back, smiled in Jessy's direction, and said, "Well. I think we can all agree: this is incredible progress!"

Along with the other board members, Jessy stood. She attempted to suppress the smile stretching across her face. When the last member had left the room, she faced her boss, who greeted her with a look that encapsulated how she felt: euphoric, relieved, and successful. "Wow—that went great! I think we'll need you at all future board meetings." Jessy felt her euphoria beginning to deflate, but just for a second. She swallowed away her self-doubt, and flashed to the experience that just occurred in this very room. The board had enthusiastically received her information, and her delivery would serve as inspiration to the younger associates in the firm. Without another thought, Jessy said, "Bring it on. I'm game!"

::

Like Jessy, you've likely felt wracked by nerves. The reality is that even the most confident of speakers gets the jitters. As Stanford communications professor Matt Abrahams says, "Research tells us that 85% of people feel nervous in high-stakes speaking situations. And quite frankly, I think the other 15% are lying."[26]

In fact, there is a biological, evolutionary need for this fear.[27] It even contains great benefits such as:

- Helping us to stay on our toes
- Inspiring us to be prepared
- Infusing us with energy

So, how did Jessy do it?

Let's review how she managed her nerves by employing the following tactics:

- She reached out to a trusted friend
- She knew her material backwards and forwards
- She focused on her listeners' needs
- She visualized the impact she would have on those that are younger

Our nervous system is here to stay, but if you can acknowledge its benefits and manage its impact, rather than try to eliminate anxiety altogether, you'll reap the rewards of getting over these great hurdles.

Based on my experience coaching more than 2,000 people through nail-biting situations, these are the top strategies that work to mitigate nerves:

---

26 Abrahams, Matt. "High-Stakes Communication: How to Manage Anxiety Speaking in Front of Others." *Insights by Stanford Business*, 7 May 2020.

27 Mobbs, Dean, et al. "The Ecology of Human Fear: Survival Optimization and the Nervous System." *Frontiers in Neuroscience*, 18 Mar. 2018.

Cognitive Strategies

1. Play your fears out to "the end"

Ask, "What's the worst that can happen? And then what? And then what?" Continue until you reach the proverbial end. The benefit of this exercise is simple: the worst-case scenario, while awful, is usually somewhat manageable. The process of identifying the worst outcome makes it more tolerable. Plus, this practice often adds levity and perspective to our fear.

2. Visualize success

Many professional athletes attribute their wins to visualizing success, and research supports their claims. In fact, let's try it here. Think about sucking on a lemon. What happens to your body? Do you feel the salivary glands in your mouth engage? Our minds are powerful tools, and we can put that to use when we prepare to speak up.

In the days (or nights!) before your presentation, envision your success. Get specific and include as many details as possible. Imagine what you will see, hear, and feel.

Start with the room. What does it look like? Visualize both the physical space as well as the people in it. Picture your own presence, standing tall. Envision what your listeners are wearing. Think about the expressions on their faces. Imagine how they look when they respond positively to what you tell them. Do they show their response by nodding their heads? By smiling? By taking notes? By asking follow-up questions?

Incorporate your other senses. What do you hear? The ticking of a clock? The humming of an AC unit? The typing of keys on a laptop?

What do you feel? Are you sitting squarely in your chair with your hands on the table? Or are you standing at a podium with your feet grounded to the floor?

The more specific your visualization, the more powerful it is.

An alternative way to use the power of visualization is to reflect on a time when you felt confident. Unearth those memories and channel that feeling—when you felt successful and on top of the world.

3. Acknowledge and welcome the nerves

Julie, a cyclist friend of mine, exemplifies this practice. She visualizes herself piloting a multi-seated bicycle with her inner critic on one seat, her inner wisdom on another, as they roll through life together singing, "We are Family."

Similarly, Elizabeth Gilbert talks about allowing fear to ride in the car on a road trip, but not letting it sit shotgun, control the radio, or pick out the snacks.

After you acknowledge your fear, try to thank it! It may sound silly, but nerves provide energy and can prevent you from sounding flat or bored when you communicate. Identify how the anxiety has helped you. Perhaps even go so far as to say out loud, "Thank you, nerves, for keeping me on my toes." The benefits of gratitude are endless, and making a practice of it propels you forward with optimism for your next Speak Up opportunity.

4. Repeat a mantra

Recall your flipped script from Chapter 10 and repeat your new script as often as possible. Make it a mantra, and your personal mission statement.

5. Savor Speak Up opportunities

You are sharing important, meaningful work with the world. Visualize what the 10-year-old you would think. Imagine how communicating well will impact younger people in your company. Have fun speaking up!

Physical Strategies

1. Power pose

A power pose is a stance that a person adopts when they're preparing to feel confident. As social psychologist Amy Cuddy describes in her 2012 TED Talk, "Your Body Language May Shape Who You Are," when you stand in a physically powerful position, you physiologically feel stronger and behave more persuasively. Although the research has been disputed, when I or my clients stand in a power pose with the intent to feel confident, we absolutely do.

The instructions for power posing are listed in Exercise 4. While I recommend doing this in a private area (like in the bathroom or in your office) rather than in front of your listeners, you can also power pose in your office chair by sitting tall with your shoulders back and your head held high.

2. Slow, deep breaths

When practiced properly, diaphragmatic breathing (from deep in your belly) can be a powerful tool in lowering heart rate. A useful technique is the Square Breathing method, described in Exercise 5. This tried-and-true practice will calm your jitters while focusing your mind (away from those pesky self-critical thoughts).

3. Physically ground yourself

Another method for combating nerves is to focus on grounding your feet into the floor or into the Earth. There are two benefits to grounding your body.

First, you feel connected to something bigger than yourself. This creates perspective (we are so small!) and can be calming to the nervous system. Second, when you stand grounded to the Earth, you feel and appear physically confident. This also holds true when you anchor your feet while seated.

Audience-Focused Strategies

1. Get curious

Rather than worrying, “What if I stumble on my words?” or “Who am I to be up here?” aim for an inquiring mind. Try asking yourself: “I wonder how they will use this information?” or “I wonder what part will be most impactful to them?”

Getting curious about your listeners helps you quiet the inner swirling of invasive thinking. When you focus on who is there with you in the room, what they care about, and how you can provide information that's relevant, you are actively redirecting your thoughts and will experience less self-criticism.

At the beginning of your Speak Up opportunity, get present. Spend some time chatting up your listeners. *Why are they attending the meeting? Do they have a nearby favorite restaurant? And how about that World Series game last night?* As a bonus, this strategy can help create connection and will further engage your listeners throughout your presentation.

2. Tap into the support of your audience

Remember, your listeners are not there to tear you apart. They are there to learn from you, and to hear your voice. When a co-worker gives an incorrect answer during a meeting, you would never berate them for it. Yet, too often as a species, we humans are harder on ourselves than on those around us. Try to offer yourself the same compassion you would give to a friend or colleague. Believe me, a little empathy goes a long way.

When You Blank Out During a Presentation

Okay. You're prepared. You followed the nerve strategies, you start to present, and—bam! You blank out. You panic. You have no idea what to say next. Here are a couple strategies to handle those out of body experiences:

1. Take a breath

What feels like a crisis in your body and in your mind is likely only a short blip, barely perceptible to your audience. Breathe to re-oxygenate your brain, settle your nerves, and recall where you were.

2. Repeat what you just said

Matt Abrahams, a professor of communication at Stanford, shares the following tactic: "Go backward to go forward." By repeating what you just said, you buy yourself some time, reminding yourself of what you were discussing. And, as a bonus, your listeners benefit from hearing the information twice.

3. Know your key messages cold

When you craft and memorize three concise messages, you can rely on those to get back into the game and out of your head. To do so, stop, take a breath, then remind your listeners of one or more of your key messages. For example, if you are deep into a discussion about how much money is needed to develop a formal mentoring program when your mind goes blank, you can say, "What's most important is that a mentoring program will save us money in the long term."

Someone once said something along the lines of, "Do one thing every day that scares you." And there's a reason this quote has so heavily made the rounds. We all have fear, every one of us. We all experience nervousness. It's a weekly (sometimes daily) recommitment to work through that fear—to speak up—but there's no question of the benefits on the other side.

> **"Playing big is being more loyal to your dreams than to your fears."**
>
> TARA MOHR

EXERCISES

Exercise 1: Examine Your Nerves

What: Look at your nerves rationally

Why: Examining your nerves helps you determine what is worth fretting over and what isn't.

How: In your journal, answer the following questions:

- When you feel nervous before you communicate, what worries you?
- Are your fears warranted?
- If you could time travel, how would you feel about this fear-inducing situation in 1 month? 6 months? 1 year? 5 years?

...

Exercise 2: Play with Your Fear

What: An exercise to see your fears in a lighthearted way.

Why: We often take ourselves too seriously, making a situation feel worse than it is.

How: Identify a fear. For example, "If I mess up this presentation, I will get fired." Play that fear out to the end.

- What's the worst that can happen? (Example: I will get fired, or I'll look stupid.)
- And then what? (Example: I won't have any money, or my colleagues won't respect me.)
- And then what? (Example: I'll have to move back in with my parents, or I'll be embarrassed every time I see them.)
- And then what? (Example: My friends and family will think I'm a loser, or I'll have to work twice as hard to make sure I regain their respect.)
- And then what?

Continue until you reach the end of your fear. How do you feel about it now? Repeat with every fear that arises.

Exercise 3: Visualize Success

What: Using as many details as possible, visualize a successful ending to your next presentation.

Why: Visualization helps you "practice" success.

How: Describe how you will make your next communication successful. Be specific. For example:

- I reserve 15 minutes in my calendar before the all-team meeting to focus on my breathing, and to remind myself what the team needs to hear.
- I review and repeat the three key messages I plan to share.
- As the meeting starts, I focus on my breath and listen for opportunities to insert my key messages.
- When the lead asks, "Are there areas we have not covered today?" I sit up straight, take a breath, then calmly say, "Yes. Based on the analysis I have conducted over the past two weeks, we have an opportunity to connect with a new demographic."
- I notice team members nodding, encouraging me to continue.
- I clearly share the next step for connecting with the new demographic and watch as the team nods.
- They ask clarifying questions for which I have solid answers.
- At the end I feel jubilant, accomplished, and validated.

While you are speaking up,:

- What do you say?
- How do you feel?
- How do you look?
- What do you hear?
- What do you see?

Think about your listeners.

- How do they react?
- What do they say?
- How do they look?

What happens as a result of this communication? Get specific.

For example, "At the end of the team meeting, I sent an email to the team, emphasizing the main idea and the next steps. Members of the team responded positively and offered assistance about how to proceed. At the next meeting, my idea was incorporated as part of the team's upcoming plans."

Write these results in your journal.

As you go into your next nerve-wracking Speak Up opportunity, channel this visualization and remind yourself, "I have visualized success. I know how this experience ends."

Exercise 4: Power Pose

What: Power pose practice.

Why: People who adopt a powerful position before speaking feel more confident. Some research confirms this, and my clients and I agree—it works!

How:

1. Stand with your feet hip-distance apart, knees slightly bent.
2. Engage your abdomen and relax your shoulders and neck.
3. Choose the pose you want to create:
   - "Wonder Woman" with your hands placed firmly on your hips,
   - "Victory Pose" with your arms raised above head in the position of a "V," or
   - "The Executive" with your hands interlaced behind your head (think of the image of the executive resting his feet on his desk and his hands cradling the back of his head).

Hold this position for two minutes. Note: two minutes in this position is longer than it feels! During the two minutes you may want to alternate your arm position by holding your arms in the Victory Pose, then The Executive, then in the Wonder Woman pose.

Exercise 5: Square Breathing

What: Practice a useful breathing method.

Why: Slow breaths, particularly exhales from deep in your belly, calm both your nervous system and mind.

How: Square breathing method:

1. Inhale for 3-4 counts.
2. Hold the inhale for 3-4 counts.
3. Exhale for 3-4 counts.
4. Rest for 3-4 counts.

Exercise 6: Physically Ground

What: An opportunity to experience the power of grounding.

Why: When we are connected to the Earth, we look and feel more confident.

How:

1. Stand with your feet hip-distance apart, knees slightly bent.
2. Engage your abdomen, roll your shoulders back, and relax your neck.
3. Take a few breaths, focusing on your connection to the Earth below. Imagine the ground supporting you in mind, body, and spirit.
4. Notice how your body feels.
5. Repeat this exercise while you are sitting.

Note: to achieve the full energetic benefits, do this exercise barefoot, which is easier to do when you work from home!

CHAPTER 12

Rehearse

Throughout her life, Zahara has been passionate about her love for the planet. In third grade, she started a lunch composting program. In high school, she worked with the school district to provide farm-to-school meal options and, in college, she advocated for a car-free campus.

So it didn't come as a surprise that she followed her childhood passion for the environment into a career focused on corporate sustainability. During her seven-year tenure at Essentials, a large household product company, Zahara climbed the career ladder to the position of director of sustainability.

As director, Zahara's goal was to reduce Essentials' carbon footprint. In order to do so, she needed buy-in from the company's top leaders. So, when she was asked to virtually present to the leadership team, she was ecstatic.

Zahara is a perfectionist, and she planned to craft a tight presentation. She spent dozens of hours creating a story that highlighted benefits for the leadership team. She spent even more time designing alluring slides that featured how Essentials would benefit by focusing on sustainability.

Next, she wrote her script, running each word through a thesaurus until her language was smooth and flowed with ease. She read and practiced every line for hours, recording "takes" long into the night.

She also rehearsed her physical movements, inserting purposeful pauses and punctuating each slide with distinct gestures.

Zahara knew that at Essentials, image was of the utmost importance. The executive team bucked the stodgy consumer packaged goods stereotype and welcomed younger, more hip leaders with innovative ideas. She planned the perfect look: a pleather tank top under a tailored blazer that was frayed at the edges, paired with her flawlessly-coiled curls.

On the day of the presentation, she felt great; her slides were polished, her script was memorized, and she looked the part. She was ready.

When it was her turn to present, Zahara smiled tightly while her eyes scanned the faces on the screen. Though her slides and script were impeccable, something was off. Despite her strong passion for sustainability, her presentation lacked the human connectedness we feel from people who speak from their heart. The genuine expression that shines through when a speaker shares an authentic story was replaced by a frozen mask. Zahara's eyes appeared dull as if she were looking right through the audience and, as a result, she appeared disinterested.

Zahara made a common mistake of presenters: she prioritized perfection over connection. She was so focused on every word that she missed the opportunity to engage the individuals in the room. As a result, the leadership team listened politely, asked a few questions, then punted the idea. Deflated, Zahara left the meeting without advancing her objective.

Afterwards, she talked with Tracy, a team member who supported Zahara's ideas. "The main problem," Tracy summarized, "is that you came across as inauthentic, too polished. After you left the meeting, I had a hard time convincing the team that you truly believed in your own presentation."

Zahara was stunned. She supported the idea of corporate sustainability, deep in her bones, and could not believe her passion was not evident. Yet when she watched the recording of the meeting, she saw what the leadership team had experienced: a perfectly executed presentation that lacked connection and relatability. She looked like she was acting, rather than persuading. Zahara was disappointed. It had taken her years to earn an opportunity to present to the leadership team. She realized that although preparation is helpful, her hyper-focus on appearing perfectly polished overshadowed the human aspects of the interaction. As a result, she was unable to convey to Essentials' leadership team her genuine passion for sustainability.

::

What. a. bummer. Putting extraordinary emphasis on every nuance and intonation of her "big day" drained the actual energy out of her presentation. Put simply, Zahara's need for perfection got the best of her.

Ironically, Zahara spends too much time over-rehearsing big opportunities and too little time preparing daily communication. This is a common—and potentially fatal—flaw. We feel too busy to rehearse and think everyday interactions like a call with a vendor, touching base with a customer or speaking at a team meeting are insignificant compared to the bigger, more important presentations. While daily communications can feel unimportant, cumulatively they contribute to the impression others have of you.

Rehearsing "smaller" communications also provides a good opportunity to improve your communication habits. And not rehearsing these means you are reinforcing the bad behaviors, like inserting fillers or qualifying statements.

Reinforcing bad habits is not limited to speaking up.

::

My friend Yvette played tennis only a handful of times before joining weekend pick-up games. She taught herself ground strokes, serves, and volleys.

Fifteen years later, Yvette decided to play in a competitive league. Her just-getting-by skills worked with friends, but now she was part of a team that wanted to win. She decided it was time to invest in lessons.

When Yvette started working with a tennis pro, she learned she had been reinforcing bad behaviors she didn't even realize she had.

Over the years, she had developed poor habits, from the way she held her racket to how she served the ball. Her incorrect form made her strokes and serves less effective and, more importantly, they wreaked havoc on her back and shoulders. It was hard to change the bad behaviors that were ingrained due to years of recreational practice.

::

Similar to Yvette's tennis game, you have spent years communicating—actually, your whole entire life. Unless you rehearse your communications (and listen to the recordings), you're likely reinforcing behaviors that could be corrected with a minimal amount of attention and practice. Exercise 2 provides a quick rule book for how to rehearse and improve communication behaviors.

Rehearsal Benefits

There are several reasons why reviewing and listening to rehearsals helps. The benefits include:

1. Increasing clarity

Determine whether your information makes sense, if there are logic gaps, and where you provide too little or too much detail.

As we discussed earlier, there are many reasons why rehearsal dinner speeches stink. While most of those reasons are related to alcohol consumption and a lack of structure, they can also be distracting because they contain too much detail, have no clear point, are full of filler words, or are rambling streams of consciousness. If every wedding toast was rehearsed from start to finish, the listening experience would vastly improve.

Here's the problem: what you know is clear in *your* mind, but what you share can get muddled. Despite your brain's best-laid plans, the words don't always spill out the way you hoped. Whether you're discussing college memories or explaining a team decision, the content is clear—to you. You know the backstory, and you have the relevant components stored neatly in your brain, but your audience may not be on the same page. They don't have all the context you inherently do. This is your "curse of knowledge." Without clear structure and rehearsals, you are unlikely to speak eloquently because you're making game-time decisions about how much background to include and how much detail to provide, leaving listeners confused.

2. Removing unnecessary words

Qualifying phrases and filler words sneak into our language far more often than you think. Until you rehearse and listen to the recording, you may not realize how often you qualify statements with "I think," or "I'm no expert," or include, "just" "maybe" and "sort of." These words pollute your ideas and, worse, dent your credibility. Rehearsing is your opportunity to catch—and remove—fillers and qualifying phrases.

3. Assessing your behavior

How you appear and sound are as (if not more) important than what you say. Rehearsing provides an opportunity to test what your audience will observe—with both their eyes and ears —and ensure you create a solid impression.

4. Determining timing

It's hard to gauge how long it will take to cover all your content. And if you have a tendency to bury the lede or provide too many details, you risk boring your audience or running out of time before you share the most important points. The last thing you want is to cram a 15-minute presentation into a 10-minute time slot.

5. Improving over time

Rehearsing is like making pancakes. The first one rarely comes out right. Either the griddle is not hot enough and the pancake winds up pale and undercooked, or it's too hot, the butter has burned, and you scorch the heck out of your breakfast. But just wait. The second (and subsequent) pancakes are always better than the first: just the right temperature, and with a golden-brown finish. So be like a pancake—*but not the first one*. Always give your audience your rehearsed version. As I say in my workshops, whether or not you make the time for it you *will* rehearse, but sometimes your rehearsal is in front of your intended listener.

How to Rehearse

Arlyne Jordan, the mother of Barbara Jordan (the U.S. Congresswoman referenced in Chapter 5), was also an impressive speaker. She "studied and imitated [role] models to discern their features, internalize their form and signal characteristics, and then, with increasing sophistication, make them her own."[28] Absorbing and personalizing your content are key to being a strong communicator.

The essence of rehearsing boils down to this: before you communicate anything, whether high stakes or everyday information, **distill your content into three key messages and internalize them**. When you know your key messages cold, you can provide a quick overview of your ideas or discuss each point at length. And, if you get distracted by a question or by someone arriving late to the meeting, you can return to those messages to remind your listeners about the essence of your ideas without getting tripped up.

The goal is to make every communication sound like a conversation, not a presentation. It's crucial you know your content well enough to create genuine interaction with the audience but never so well that your communication becomes a performance.

To do this, practice with an outline, then share your key messages in various ways to make sure you demonstrate your intent and that your listeners can clearly pick up your most important points.

28 Google book about Arlyne Jordan

Here are specific techniques for rehearsing the range of communication you will deliver, from everyday to high stakes.

How to Rehearse a Meeting Update

1. Create an outline

Rather than scripting your meeting update, create an outline using key words to represent the content you plan to share.

Using the template helps in many ways including to:

- Structure your content in a clear way
- See the big picture, rather than get lost in the weeds
- Keep you organized and calm your mind
- Keep your audience tracking what you share with them
- View your entire content, distilled into key words, on a single page

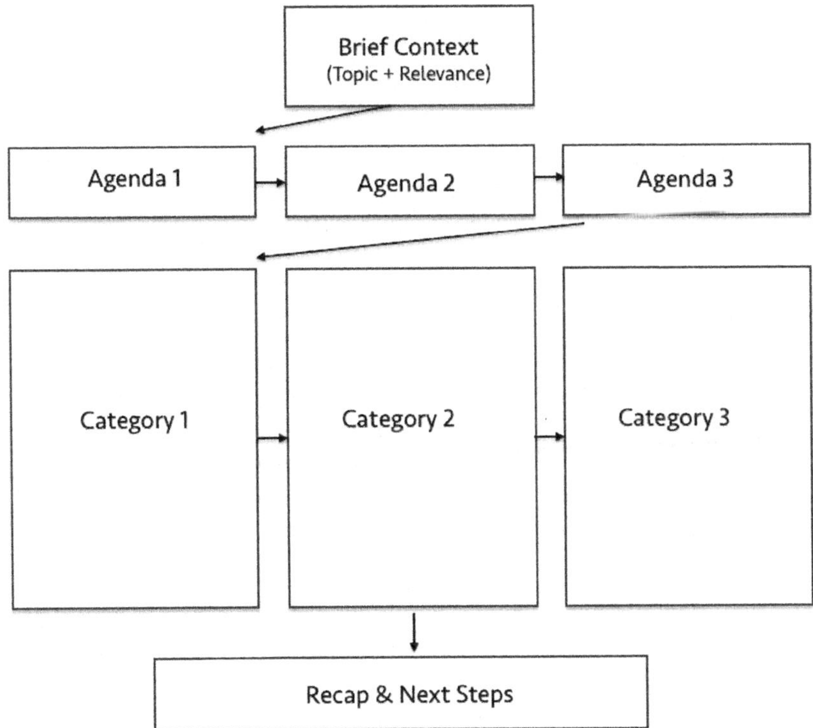

The different components of the outline include:

Context: Briefly name your topic, and why it's important to your audience.

Agenda: Provide a *brief* agenda (simply name the categories you will discuss) to prepare your listeners for what they are about to hear.

Category: Provide details about the three sections of your topic.

Recap & Next Steps: Provide a brief reminder about what you discussed and what the next steps are.

Here is a client's update focused on how to add more employees to their growing start-up:

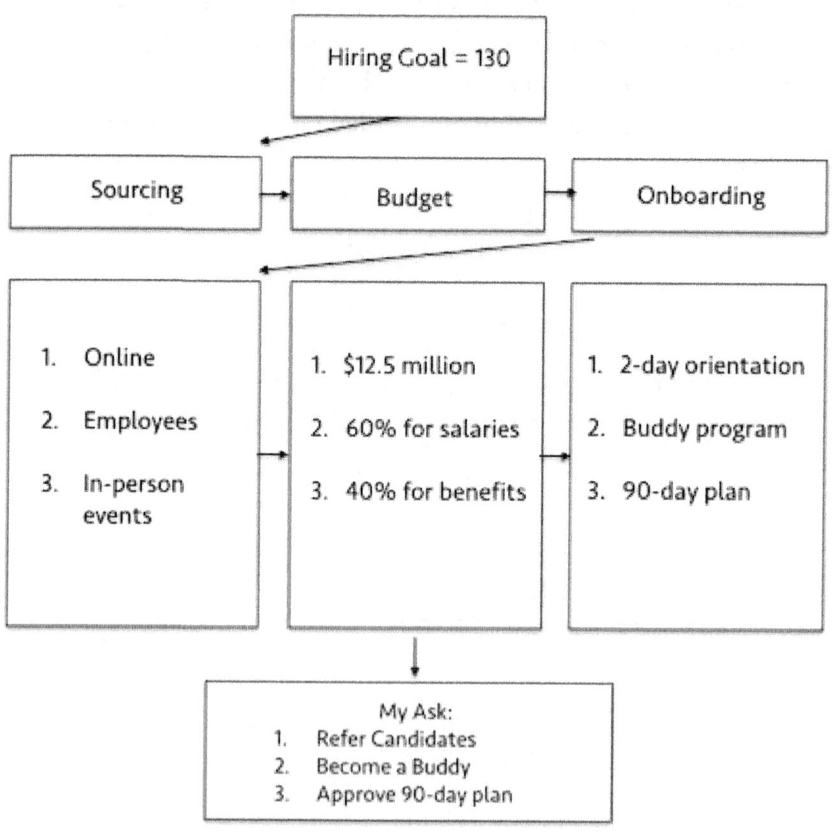

To see an example of what you might say, see the table below. Note, this is sample language and not intended to be a script. In other words, resist the temptation to write your sentences out.

Outline Area	Key Words	What You Might Say (Note: this is not a script!)
Context	Hiring goal = 130 people	As you may know, we have an ambitious internal growth goal as we hope to hire 130 people in the upcoming year.
Agenda	Sourcing, Budget, Onboarding	Today I'll share the plan to meet this goal as it relates to sourcing employees, the budget needed, and onboarding new hires.
Category One:	Sourcing: 1. Online 2. Employees 3. In-person events	Since we are in a competitive job market, we need to be creative and thorough about sourcing candidates. We have a three-pronged approach for finding candidates: 1. Online job sites and social media 2. Employee referrals and incentive programs 3. In-person events such as college job fairs, general career fairs, and tech-focused conferences
Category Two:	Budget: $12.5 million 60% salaries 40% benefits	130 new hires will cost the company 12.5 million dollars in salary and benefits. 60% of that number goes to paying salaries and 40% to paying benefits. The finance team has confirmed we have the budget.

Outline Area	Key Words	What You Might Say (Note: this is not a script!)
Category Three:	Onboarding: 1. 2-day orientation 2. Buddy program 3. 90-day plan	The Talent Development team is updating the company onboarding process in three ways by: 1. Creating a 2-day orientation program that educates new hires about all the aspects of our company 2. Starting a new buddy system so new hires have a person—in addition to their manager—who can show them the ropes and answer their questions 3. Outlining specific activities for new hires and their managers for the first 90 days. While the activities will add to your already busy calendars, the investment of time will pay off once the new hires are fully onboarded
Recap & Next Steps	Ask: • Candidates • Buddy • Support 90-day plan	As senior leaders in the organization, we ask you to: • Examine your networks for candidates and send those names to our recruiters • Sign up to be a buddy • Complete the activities listed in the 90-day plan

2. Record and listen

Audio record a rehearsal using your outline to guide you. Don't worry. This can be what I lovingly refer to as your "Shitty First Draft."

3. Rehearse in front of a friend or co-worker

Time to get to work! Rehearse in person, ideally in front of a target audience member who will give you feedback.

How to Rehearse with Slides

1. Start with the outline template. Your outline is a method for seeing the big picture, which is the key first step to internalize your content and communication flow.
2. Identify the key points you want to make on each slide.
3. Practice speaking to the audience rather than the slides. Too often we look exclusively at our slides as if the answers are embedded there on the screen.

Exercise 4 details all the steps for rehearsing with slides.

Overcome Rehearsing Resistance

If you're like most of my clients, you hate rehearsing. I'll let you in on a secret, I don't love it either. One of the stall tactics I (and others) use is to edit and revise each slide and each point. To overcome your resistance, play the "90-Second Game." Exercise 3 provides the details for how to play. This process is a summary of your presentation and helps you to identify and internalize your key messages *and* warms you up before you dive into a more thorough rehearsal. Plus, let's be honest. Doesn't playing a game sound much more interesting than rehearsing?

Best Rehearsal Strategies

Regardless of whether you are preparing for a short meeting update or a long, formal onstage presentation, it's important to do the following:

1. Rehearse out loud

That may seem silly or obvious, but many people tell me they click through their slides and think about what they will say on each slide. *This is not a rehearsal.* To effectively communicate, you must practice by speaking out loud.

2. Practice the first 60+ seconds

Know your opening, cold. Identify the habits that emerge when you are nervous, then rehearse while over-exaggerating the opposite behaviors. For example, if you increase your pace when you're nervous, slowwww down and over enunciate words, incorporating long pauses at regular intervals.

3. Hold eye contact with a friendly face

Your friendly face can be with a live person or a representation of a happy listener; a smiley face drawn on a sticky note will work. Maintain eye contact while you rehearse, just as you will do during the real thing.

4. Close strong

The opening and closing are when your listeners pay the most attention. Too often my clients end their communication by trailing off, ending abruptly, or tossing in a weak "thank you." Since your closing represents valuable "real estate," rehearse a closing that reinforces your key messages, the next steps, or serves as a reminder for why your listeners will find this content pertinent.

5. Develop transitions

This is where speakers often stumble because we forget to prepare transition statements. Instead, most listeners transition with a loud "ummm." Practice recapping the main point of each slide and highlighting how that information relates to the subsequent slide.

6. Be a good storyteller

Few of us have patience for a long, drawn-out story but we all appreciate when the length is just right, and it contains interesting details.

Finally, you should practice connecting with your listeners by:

- Smiling within the first 30 seconds. (Bonus: smiling dissolves the tension in your body.)

- Asking a question, placing the focus on *them* and away from yourself.

Should I Memorize a Script?

A frequent question I receive is, "Should I memorize a script?" In a word: NO. Why?

1. You can't be emotionally present. When you script and memorize your communication, you're focused on the specific words and the exact piece of information that comes next. Your audience can tell you're not truly seeing them nor present in the moment.
2. You can't genuinely connect to the audience nor adapt to their reactions. As mentioned in the Eye Contact chapter, it's important to look at your audience to gauge their understanding and interest. Based on what you see, you should adapt by either explaining in a different way, adapting your vocal and visual style, cutting to the chase, or stopping to allow your listeners to ask questions. Having an outline gives you the flexibility to adapt to your audience while staying on track.
3. You put pressure on yourself to get it exactly right. That self-induced constraint, combined with the intensity of showing up in the room, is too big of a cognitive load. When you mess up (note that I say "when" because we all do), you will notice the mistake, overreact to it, and show your listeners you jumbled your script. Trust me. They'll notice.
4. Your Q&A style will sound different. Shifting from the role of a proficient communicator during your presentation to a hesitant one during Q&A casts doubts about your authenticity. Your goal is to demonstrate your genuine style during your communication *and* during Q&A.
5. Your time is valuable. Writing and memorizing requires time that would be better spent rehearsing with an outline.

The bottom line? Memorizing and over-rehearsing is our way to control the situation. As in many sports like rowing, tennis, or golf, holding on too tightly to the oar, racket, or club makes you tense and your strokes worse. Despite your desire to hold on to your presentation for dear life, loosen your grip to make your communication more authentic. Counterintuitively, this will also make you appear more confident.

EXERCISES

Exercise 1: The 90-Second Game

What: A game to make rehearsing easy and fun.

Why: We often avoid rehearsing because it feels overwhelming, hard, or awkward. The 90-second game reduces those barriers.

How:

1. Fill in the eight boxes in the outline worksheet detailed on page 157 and also available at www.hopetimberlake.com/exercises.
2. Using the one-page outline, share an approximate 90 second summary of your topic. The goal is to speak your main ideas aloud with enough context and detail so that listeners hear your perspective but without too many details to bog you (or them) down.

Exercise 2: Rehearse Your Next Meeting

What: An opportunity to practice rehearsing an everyday meeting.

Why: We rarely practice everyday meetings even though these, cumulatively, impact our career more than our less frequent higher-stakes meetings.

How:

1. Use your phone or a teleconferencing program like Zoom to record a rehearsal of your next meeting update.

2. Watch and listen to the recording to determine if you like what you see and hear.
3. Repeat until you feel ready to contribute at your next meeting.

Exercise 3: PowerPoint Karaoke

What: A fun way to practice speaking spontaneously.

Why: Learning how to speak to material you have not yet seen or rehearsed is a good skill.

How: PowerPoint karaoke is a game where the presenter is introduced to a bizarre slide deck they've never seen before and is then expected to stand up and present. This is a great game to strengthen your skills of improvisation. It's also helpful to practice viewing the slide, absorbing the content, then engaging with your audience while you talk about it.

1. Go to hopetimberlake.com/exercises to access karaoke slides or search "PowerPoint karaoke slides" online.
2. Find a friend or colleague—the more the better—to watch you present. If you cannot find an audience, you can play by yourself.
3. As you present, note how often you look at the slides.

Bonus: audio-record yourself, then listen to the recording. Compare how uncomfortable and awkward you *felt* while speaking about the random presentation but how much better you sound than you felt in the moment.

Exercise 4: Rehearse with Slides

1. Start with the outline template on page 157 and also available at www.hopetimberlake.com/exercises. You may have more slides than what is represented in the outline. For example, you may have slides that represent a creative opening or stories. *Do not fret!* Your outline is a method for seeing the big picture, which is a key first step to internalize your content and communication flow.

2. Identify the key points you want to make on each slide. There should be a limited number of points on each slide, ideally no more than three and never more than five. If you have more than five points per slide, make sure your listeners need (and want) to hear all of them. If all of your points are truly relevant to your listeners, combine points into fewer "buckets" of information.

   For example, if you plan to talk about marketing tactics for reaching customers and want to include Instagram updates, Facebook ads, email campaigns, Yelp promotions, Google search, and customer referral programs, you'll want to categorize the six items into fewer buckets. You could talk about Web-based Strategies (Instagram, Facebook, Google, and Yelp) and Email Strategies (campaigns and customer referral programs).

   Alternatively, you could add another slide, so you don't overwhelm your audience by sharing too much information on each one. For additional slide tips, refer to Nancy Duarte's *Slideology*.

3. Once you've identified the key points on each slide, create a sticky note that will contain key word(s) to remind you of what you plan to say for each one.

   If you are viewing speaker notes during your presentation, type the number of points you want to make (1-5) and write a key word(s) next to each. Quantifying the number is helpful as it creates a structure (within a structure!). As we discussed earlier, structure helps you internalize the content, and provides peace of mind.

4. Print out the slides and number them on the bottom left corner. Next, place the sticky note on each slide. Place a second sticky note (ideally using a different color or at least a different color pen) and write a large "T" for transition on the top. Then, write a few key words—not a complete sentence—to remind you of how you plan to transition from one slide to another. These transition sticky notes go on the bottom right-hand corner.
5. Tape the slides to a wall. Rehearse your content in its entirety looking at just the slides and sticky notes, i.e., ignore your computer altogether. Audio record rehearsals and be sure to listen to them closely. You didn't do all this work for nothing!

CHAPTER 13

Complications

Sai was just 23 when she moved from India to New York City to attend graduate school at NYU. She was initially overwhelmed by the city's cost of living and the rude people she occasionally encountered. But she soon adjusted to—and fell in love with—the energy and pace of Manhattan.

After earning her Master in Technology Management, Sai could not wait to become a project manager. Unfortunately, finding her first job was not a simple task, but she was not deterred. During each interview, Sai spoke about her training, experience, and capabilities with enthusiasm.

Months later, when Sai was finally hired as a project manager, she felt ecstatic. All the time and energy she'd spent in school, taking part in internships, and looking for a job had really paid off.

Her excitement quickly faded when Sai overheard a group of five men criticizing her, not because she was a woman nor because she was the only Indian individual on the team, but because she appeared too young. They could not understand how Sai could oversee their project and, in a sense, oversee *them*.

One Friday, late in the afternoon, Sai's manager checked in with her about the project. Sai had been keeping it together, but when her manager asked how she was doing, she shared the negative feedback she'd overheard and broke down. Sai did her best to reassure her manager that she had the situation under control. In return, he calmed her down saying, "Don't worry. You're doing great."

Sai felt so much better, comforted by her supportive manager, and spent the weekend confident that everything would be fine.

On Monday when she returned to work, she received a call from human resources saying, "You're very good at what you do. Your skills are solid—but you should not be a project manager."

One month into her dream job, Sai was basically fired. The news left her shattered.

What they offered her instead was a different role that was unrelated to her training in project management. The demotion stung, as did the $20,000 salary haircut. Without irony, Sai was told that, in addition to her full-time job, she was "allowed" to shadow other project managers to learn the ropes. Without compensation.

Sai quickly moved from her dream role to a lesser paying, more irrelevant job with the option to spend dozens of hours shadowing a project manager—for free. She was tempted to turn down the demotion, but she was on a work visa. She needed to pay her rent, and had too many dependencies to jump back into the job market.

Begrudgingly, Sai began her new job wondering why she had even bothered to earn a technology management degree from NYU. This felt like a career setback, and it was exhausting having to invest extra hours while not getting paid.

But that was Sai's perspective on a bad day. On a good day, she realized it offered her an opportunity.

Months into her new dual-role, Sai started applying to project manager positions. She was excited about the prospect of finding a job that matched her goals, but her inner self kept saying, "Do you even know what you're doing? You barely have any experience—and you were demoted after only one month."

Still, Sai was determined. She updated her skills on LinkedIn and applied to dozens of jobs. She was honest about her career setback and, again, faced some rejection. But seven months after her demotion, she was offered a project manager job at twice her current salary, and $30,000 more than her original position.

She felt exhausted and whiplashed, but Sai was ecstatic. Five years later, she's become a respected project manager, receiving regular promotions and serving as a model to younger women in her organization.

::

Like Sai, you may sometimes face setbacks when you speak up. You may be interrupted, ignored, or, in Sai's case, may proactively share your abilities only to be demoted a month later. It's frustrating (and scary) to develop the courage and the skills to use your voice, only to then be thwarted.

My advice? *Keep trying.*

Here are some complications you've likely faced and what you can do to circumvent these obstacles:

They don't listen to you

Have you ever attended a meeting where you begin talking, look around the room, and realize no one is paying attention? Your listeners are looking at their phones, avoiding eye contact, or otherwise not responding to the information you share.

Solutions:

Assess *what* information you shared and *how* you shared it. To engage your listeners, make sure you do the following.

1. Share audience-relevant content.
2. Use compelling words like benefit, savings, and innovation.
3. Show your passion.

Your listeners interrupt or talk over you

Having people interrupt and talk over you is frustrating and downright rude—and it happens all the time.

Solutions:

1. Outline your content at the start of your communication, e.g., "Today I'm going to share the status of our work in Haiti, review next steps, and allot time for questions at the end."
2. Quantify your topics, e.g., "There are 2 project updates and 4 next steps."
3. Share your expectations with your listeners, e.g., "Since we have a lot to cover in one hour, please save your questions and feedback until the end."

When you provide an overview, quantify your topics, and establish expectations, you have grounds to stop interruptions. Plus, you've set the groundwork for other listeners to speak up on your behalf. *("George, she said she'll take comments at the end.")*

When these strategies are ineffective at warding off interrupters, prepare an assertive phrase that indicates you are not yet finished. Feel free to channel those you admire, those with a strong voice. During her debate with Vice President Mike Pence, Kamala Harris's brilliant and sharp delivery of "I'm speaking" is one example of a statement you can make to hold on to the floor.

Exercise 2 provides examples of each strategy and an opportunity to practice.

Mansplaining and he-peating

As you likely already know, "mansplaining" refers to when a man explains something as if you could not possibly know the information without his assistance.

Similarly, "he-peating" is when someone in the room repeats an idea you previously shared, communicating as if it is their own.

Based on the names of these phenomena, we presume men are the culprits though these techniques have been used by all overbearing colleagues.

Regardless of who the offender is, neither complication feels good!

Solutions:

1. **Respond graciously**

Convey your sincerity in your response.

Sample responses
"Thank you, Jack. As it turns out, I read profit and loss statements all the time, but I appreciate knowing who to turn to if I have questions," or "Brin, thank you for backing up what I said earlier. I'm glad we're on the same page."

Benefits
- Maintains a positive relationship with the offender.
- Reinforces your ideas and capabilities.
- Demonstrates that you don't lose your cool.

Risks
- You may feel frustrated and may not prevent future mansplaining or he-peating.

2. **Regain the floor**

Clearly communicate your position. Questions help engage the offender and can make it easier to employ this strategy.

Sample responses
"Thank you for recapping what I mentioned earlier. Does anyone need further clarification about the topic?" or "Yes, Raj, that is the essence of what I proposed at the start of the meeting, but the part you missed was . . . " or "I appreciate you summarizing my thoughts. Is there an additional point you want to make?"

Benefits
- Reinforces your ideas and capabilities.
- Asserts yourself as the one communicating.

Risks
- It's hard to do this in a calm manner.

- It can appear condescending if worded poorly.
- You may lose your cool and lose credibility as well.

Pro Tip: Anticipate and rehearse a clear, assertive response. One client's go-to strategy? "Smile kindly and say, 'That's a good way of re-stating what I said.'" Exercise 2 provides an opportunity to practice.

3. Respond sarcastically or playfully

Sample responses
"Wow, Jack. It's amazing; I've been in the finance department for five years and did not know how to read a profit and loss statement until you explained it to me." or "Marcos, did you really think I couldn't interpret a profit and loss statement after all these years of working together?"

Benefits
- You feel good standing up for yourself.

Risks
- The relationship could falter, and you can face consequences, depending on who the culprit is.

4. The ally strategy

Make a pact with other colleagues who will be willing to stick up for you or "call out" the behavior. This effort is not meant to be in spite, but can actually be viewed as a vote of confidence and support. And perhaps the offender will learn something, and think better about their actions next time. As the saying goes, "a rising tide lifts all boats."

Sample responses
"Great idea, right, Noam? I loved it when Celeste first proposed it." or "Jack, all of us have worked in the accounting department for years. Everyone knows how to interpret profit and loss statements."

Benefits

- Consensus is more powerful than a one-on-one debate.

Risks

- The allies in the room may feel too intimidated to speak up.

CLIENT PERSPECTIVE

"Allies are important for minority groups. It's easy to gravitate towards people who are similar to you because it feels safer but it's very important not to stay in your comfort zone. You need someone who can speak on your behalf who is in the majority."

Vulnerability Hangover

Since my 2017 enrollment in Tara Mohr's *Playing Big* course, I have intentionally made leaps in my professional life. This includes speaking on podcasts, presenting on stages, leading large virtual workshops, and sharing ideas on social media. The good news? These opportunities usually go well. In fact, the consistent feedback I receive is flattering, and also validating. Yet, after each of these opportunities, I still find myself awake at 2 am, reliving the event. Instead of savoring it, I lie there in the dark, rehashing every little detail I may have gotten wrong.

- Did I listen closely enough to that question? Or answer her fully?
- Did I use the right word? Or worse, did I inadvertently offend someone in the room?
- Did I come across as credible but too stern? Or blonde and ditzy?

With these questions swirling, I ruminate over and over.

If, after speaking up, you experience what Brené Brown refers to as a "vulnerability hangover," it's important to know this is normal. Tara Mohr reassures us that as we begin to play big, our fear increases. She goes further to explain, this is our inner critic's method of trying to keep us safe. But the critic rearing its ugly head is not a sign to retreat. Instead, it's a sign we're onto something important. So, take it from me. Keep going.

If and when you experience your own post Speak Up panic, refer back to the strategies in the Self-Talk and Nerves chapters. And give yourself a giant pat on the back for putting yourself out there.

The Power of Questions

Having your ideas shot down can feel really discouraging. Rather than taking it as a blow to your ego, look at this setback as an opportunity—one that can help shed some light on what went wrong, and what can be done better. The best way to accomplish this is to get curious. Ask questions.

::

My client Selena experienced a setback a few years ago when she shifted from consulting to banking. She noticed the partners at her private equity firm didn't appear interested in her ideas or her years of experience. Frustrated, she wanted to throw in the towel and return to consulting. But after she and I spoke, Selena was able to reframe the situation.

The next time partners tried to blow her off, she asked, "Would you be open to a 15-minute conversation so I can learn about your experiences and priorities?"

The partners were eager to talk about themselves—this is true of most people, and particularly those in charge. Selena learned more about their interests, and as a result, her rapport-building effort and investigative exercises paid off.

Armed with new insights, Selena framed her ideas by showing how they aligned with and supported the partners' values.

In the three years since Selena joined the firm, she's been promoted and is considered a crucial team member.

Exercise 5 provides examples of questions you can ask, and will give you an opportunity to practice.

How Authentic Should I Be?

Authenticity is all the rage—and for good reason. After all, who wants a communicator or a leader who appears fake or disingenuous?

Here's the challenge: what does authenticity really mean? Are you most authentic when you are with your parents and grandparents? Or with your childhood friends? Or with a romantic partner? Or when you let loose on a Friday night after a long week?

The truth is, we adapt to our environment. The "you" who dances on a bar is not the "you" who shows up for Sunday family dinner nor the "you" who attends a team meeting.

And that's okay. In fact, it's career preserving.

Just like your boss's boss doesn't want to see you argue with your siblings, the company does not need to see the CEO releasing stress by meditating in his boxers.

Hilary, a senior manager at a bank, and often the only person of color in her meetings, states, "We all leave portions of our identity at the door, but we should show them the most important ones."

According to Herminia Ibarra, author of *Act Like a Leader, Think Like a Leader*, authenticity can be an excuse to hide or a reason not to improve. Rather than focusing on your true *current* self, she recommends acting like your *aspirational* authentic self. She explains, "Moving into a bigger leadership role requires people to act against their natural inclinations."

Hilary agrees. "Some days I'm going to fake it 'til I make it. I mean, don't we all?"

To determine if sharing your authentic self helps or hinders you, ask the following questions:

- Does being authentic mean showing my biggest, boldest self?
- What is the benefit for you when you bring that self to work? And for others in your workplace, and younger colleagues coming up after you?

- What is the risk? And for others in your workplace or those coming up behind you?

With more experience and seniority, you may be able to demonstrate more authenticity. Now that Hilary has a senior role and is financially stable, she can be more open and honest at work because she has options.

This is also true of Microsoft's Chief Financial Officer, Amy Hood. Earlier in her career, she worked 100 hour weeks and missed holidays with family, as well as the weddings of close friends. Now, dubbed one of the most powerful women in the world according to Fortune Magazine, Amy feels comfortable revealing her true self, and has no problem driving Microsoft employees in her minivan, laden with banana peels.

CLIENT PERSPECTIVE

Jasmin, a supply chain manager, says,

"I've been told a lot of things . . . an aggressive white manager told me to be more aggressive. A black man from Jamaica said I should speak 'the Queen's English.' Other times I want to challenge how we're always doing things, but I'm cautious about being labeled an 'angry black woman.' I have to be worried about how I'm perceived."

Do I Have to Compromise to Be Heard?

As we all know, every sector of corporate America is predominantly run by white men. Those of us who are not white and male must decide: *do I compromise how I speak up and appease the leadership?*

According to a Deloitte report, 83% of lesbian, gay, and bisexual people and 66% of women are "not themselves at work."

In Shawon Jackson's Stanford Business School keynote, "Problematizing Persuasion," he criticizes himself for falling into the trap of compromising. As he says, "Our world favors those who fit in." Yet to be authentic, Shawon contends you need to "hold true to your values" and not "compromise too much."

This is easier said than done.

As Hilary has experienced, people without privilege need to weigh the risks and rewards of speaking authentically. Even today, in her role as a manager there is a "good section of my workday where I'm playing pretend: be non-threatening, be really competent, smile, don't say this."

Circling back to the 2020 Vice Presidential debate with Kamala Harris and Mike Pence, you can imagine how much restraint it took for Kamala to turn to Pence and say, "I'm speaking," versus "Will you shut up, man?" as Joe Biden said to Donald Trump.

Women, and particularly women of color are in the double bind of needing to "be warm and conform."

There is no straightforward answer to determine how often (or specifically when) to vary your speech, but the journaling questions explored below will help you reflect on the best method for reaching your goals.

Should I Adapt My Voice?

Whether I'm coaching men or women, be it seasoned CEOs or people new to their career, I use two frames for determining how they should use their voice.

First, what do your listeners need? Are they looking for reassurance and empathy? If so, your goal is to channel vocal behaviors like a softer tone or a slower pace that allow you to both feel and display those emotions.

Next, what feels authentic to you? Like Carmela in Chapter 4, you may be fired up about an opportunity to show your chops. Yes, you could share your enthusiasm—but if you don't meet their primary need to be reassured, your listeners will simply not be open to your excitement.

Some clients note, "Whoa. Am I really supposed to adapt to *them*? What if their needs don't align with my goals?"

This is a fair question. Try to think of it this way: you're not compromising yourself but rather giving your audience what they need in order to hear what you have to say. As an example, when you are angry and need to vent, or when you take your frustration out on a pint of Ben & Jerry's, how do you feel when someone offers advice about how you *should* have handled the situation? What would be most helpful in that moment is to have their support and understanding, not their solutions.

The same holds true for your audience.

If you are excited to propose a new program to the leadership team, and they are worried about finances, you need to acknowledge their financial concern. You can do so in a soothing voice before nimbly moving on to your project.

Here is another example of adapting. My client Briana is soft-spoken, while her team is loud and animated. When it's her turn to share an update, team members tend to interrupt her, look down at their phones, or ask a question that clearly indicates they weren't listening. Although this is a very frustrating experience, Briana knows remaining on the team is the best strategy for her career. With that in mind, she channels the advice author Susan Cain provides in her book, *Quiet: The Power of Introverts in an Extroverted World*: sometimes you need to speak in a tone and manner that ensures you are heard in the meeting, even if it exhausts you to do so.

Code-Switching

Code-switching is when a speaker alternates between two or more languages, or language varieties, to build rapport and fit in. When I ask people of color, they emphatically agree that code-switching is real. We also see famous examples of code-switchers including Barack Obama and Trevor Noah.

In *Born a Crime*, Trevor Noah's biography, he says, "Language more than color defines who you are to people" He and his mother would code-switch out of necessity. For example, his mom spoke in

Afrikaans to the store owner while Trevor spoke Zulu to the neighborhood kids who tried to mug him.

Research shows, and common sense dictates, that code-switching carries with it a huge psychological burden. "The code-switching experience can feel isolating and threatening—while you are trying your best to show up as a positive, hardworking 'team player,' a part of you is in a constant state of censorship."[29] Jasmin, an "only" African American with 17 years' experience in supply chain management, says she uses slang, but not in the office. She has to think about it, but it's not a burden. And while code-switching is real, she continues, "I don't think we should bring our whole selves to work—that would be a hot mess."

As D'Arcy says to her students who resist adapting to the room's norms, "Look, this is just a tool. It isn't going to change your identity. You don't have to lose your authenticity by changing your dialect."

To get comfortable with assimilating to the corporate environment. you may need to focus on your goal for speaking up. Is it to have a seat at the table? Contribute to strategy? Make your way up the corporate ladder? While changing your voice may seem like you are compromising your identity, you need to make a decision. Do you want to work in this type of setting? If not, you have your answer. But if you think working for this company is important for financial security, future prospects, health benefits, or any number of reasons, it will be crucial you get comfortable using your voice in a way that feels heard. Just as you speak differently with friends versus family, everyone has to adjust their words for the environment they want to succeed in.

Perfectionism

Most of the obstacles in this chapter refer to speedbumps you inevitably face when speaking up. However, one of the most powerful deterrents to success is the obstacle you create for yourself: perfectionism.

---

29 Mwanza, Chanju. "The Burdens of Code-Switching between Your 'Motherland' and 'Home.'" *VERVE: She Said*, 16 May 2019.

We've seen how Zahara's quest for perfection backfired during the Rehearsal chapter, and how this behavior is problematic in every aspect of speaking up.

Experts agree about the danger of perfectionism. Minda Harts, author of *The Memo: What Women of Color Need to Know to Secure a Seat at the Table* says, "Perfectionism will stifle all your momentum. Your concept will never feel 100% baked and ready."

Diana Kapp, author of *Girls Who Run the World* agrees: "Perfectionism is for machines, not people."

To overcome perfectionism, focus on progress—even incremental progress—not precision.

"Code-switching is fun for me. I don't even do it intentionally. I just find speaking to one person, I change a few words, I change my tone, I change my accent slightly. It's a seamless transition that I do without even thinking, like a chameleon."

TREVOR NOAH

EXERCISES

Exercise 1: Ward Off Interrupters

What: Implement strategies to prevent interruptions.

Why: Interruptions occur frequently, but there are small tactics you can use to prevent them.

How: Rehearse each of these strategies before your next meeting:

1. Outline your content at the start of your communication. For example, "My update will include a brief overview of the progress made to date, a deep dive into the problems that emerged, and proposed solutions." People are less likely to interrupt if they hear an overview of what will be shared.
2. After your outline, set your expectations. For example, "I'll provide an overview of the program, and then will save time at the end for questions and discussion." By sharing the ground rules, your listeners know how to behave and, when they do interrupt, it's easier to point out that you are not finished (as in: "Frank, I'd love to address your idea once I'm finished describing the program").
3. Quantify your topics. For example, "In reviewing this account, it's important to look at three benchmarks." Continue to signpost throughout your update by saying, "The second important benchmark is . . . "
4. Craft and practice a statement to stop interrupters. Examples include: "Please let me finish" or "As soon as I am finished, I will open up the floor for discussion."

Exercise 2: Mansplain and He-peat Responses

What: Practice responses you can share when someone mansplains to you or he-peats your ideas.

Why: It's hard to respond effectively in the moment. By practicing your responses before you encounter these obstacles, you'll be better prepared to communicate clearly and confidently.

How:
1. Practice mansplain responses including the:
   - Gracious response: "While I do know how the process works, I appreciate your intention to make sure we're all on the same page," said sincerely.
   - Sarcastic response: "Although I have been overseeing the process for nine months, I never would have known how it works without you explaining it to me," said sarcastically.
   - Ally strategy: Find others who can be your allies in meetings by standing up to mansplainers.
2. Practice he-peat responses including the:
   - Collaborative response: "Thanks for summarizing my comments. I'm glad we are all clear on next steps."
   - Regain the floor response: "Thank you for circling back to my earlier point. Does anyone have a different approach or any questions?"
   - Strategic response: Find an ally with whom you can practice calling out the he-peater: "That's an interesting paraphrase. I'm glad you understood what [my ally] said."

Exercise 3: Vulnerability Hangovers

What: A journaling exercise to handle vulnerability hangovers.

Why: After you present, you may be left with a feeling of fear or a sense of vulnerability. While this is perfectly normal, it's important to identify some strategies to make sure these feelings don't prevent you from speaking up in the future.

How: Answer the following questions in your journal:

1. When was the last time you felt a vulnerability hangover? What was the situation that preceded it? What content did you share? Who was in the room? What is your relationship with them? What are your feelings towards them?
2. What did you do well in this communication? What could you improve? How would a neutral observer assess the situation?
3. What fears arose during your vulnerability hangover? Are they true?
4. Refer to the Nerve strategies in Chapter 11. Which of these strategies can help you move through these feelings? Which strategies could help reduce the hangover severity and frequency?

Exercise 4: The Power of Probing

What: Craft and practice questions you can ask to build rapport and clarify motivations.

Why: People often shoot down ideas because we don't have a strong relationship with the person presenting the idea, or the ideas don't align with our priorities. Asking questions helps both of those situations.

How: Brainstorm queries that help you build rapport and understand your listeners' motivations. Here are examples:

"How did you see this situation when you were starting out? What has changed since then?"

"What lesson have you learned over time that has served you well?"

"What would make this idea more interesting?"

"What are the reasons behind your decision?"

"How could we align this idea with the company's priorities?"

"What do you think are the most pressing concerns?"

"What are you hoping to achieve this month / quarter / year?"

Exercise 5: Authenticity

What: A journaling exercise to determine the risks and rewards of being authentic.

Why: It's hard to determine how honest and direct you should be at work. It helps to map your decision so that it aligns with your goals and the context.

How: Answer the following questions in your journal.

1. If you were completely honest at work, how would that impact:
   - Your feeling of self-worth?
   - Your career goals?
   - How people in the room view you?
   - How people in the company view you?
2. If you hid your opinions and true self at work, how would that impact:
   - Your feeling of self-worth?
   - Your career goals?
   - How people in the room view you?
   - How people in the company view you?
3. What conditions need to be in place for you to speak authentically?

Exercise 6: Perfectionism

What: A journaling exercise to determine how perfectionism impacts your speaking up.

Why: We turn to perfectionism both as a method of control and because we think it will result in a better presentation. Well, *surprise*. Research and anecdotal evidence show it doesn't!

How: Answer the following questions in your journal.

- When does perfectionism prevent you from reaching your communication goal?
- When have you trusted yourself to present without aiming for perfection?
- What would it take for you to focus on progress over perfectionism?
- Identify one scenario in which you can put perfectionism aside in order to share your voice?

Exercise 7: Wisdom to Handle Complications

What: An activity to determine how to handle complications.

Why: We often feel helpless in the face of obstacles. This activity provides insight into how to overcome them.

How:

1. Using the voice recording feature on your phone, talk about all the obstacles you face when you speak up.

   For example, you could talk about the colleague who interrupts you, your manager who does not support you, or the board room setting that intimidates you. Talk for as long as you can. Don't hold back—no one will hear your rant.

2. Take a deep breath, move to another part of the room, and now audio-record from the perspective of those who are creating the complications. Get specific about what is happening for each person. Dig deep into their frame of mind.

   Using the example above, dive into the mind of the interrupting colleague. Why does he interrupt? What's going on for him? When you have fully explained his point of view, get into the head of your manager. Why is she not supporting you? What are her goals and motivations? Finally, what is the perspective of those in the boardroom?

   Speak for as long as it takes to fully represent the perspectives of those in the room when you face obstacles.

3. Take a breath and move to a third part of the room. This time, audio record the situation from the perspective of an external observer like a consultant, coach, or mentor. What does she see when she views the situation? Get very specific and speak for as long as you can.

4. When you finish the third audio recording, write down any thoughts that emerge. Do you see your obstacles differently? Do you have new insights about how you can handle them? What can you do when you face these challenges in the future?

   Ideally, this exercise allows you to recognize that you have more agency than you thought.

CHAPTER 14

Next

The year was 1990. The style was shoulder pads and big hair (think Julia Roberts in Pretty Woman), and technology was old-school. In the 90s, video recording took place only in professional settings using large equipment that took up a lot of floor space. There were no smartphones nor small video recording devices. College kids were not content creators making TikToks in their dorm rooms. In fact, the only videos that featured students were recorded through a broadcast journalism course in a studio setting. In other words, creating videos was a big deal.

Kristina was a 19-year-old journalism student with her eye on a career in broadcasting. Though she was not even old enough to legally drink a beer, she bravely applied to host a television show through the communications department at the University of Wisconsin. The program, called "International Insights," aired weekly on a local Eau Claire station. Never mind that Kristina had never travelled outside a U.S. border, and Eau Claire was the fifth smallest TV market in the country. She was up for the challenge and responsibility of creating a show that highlighted the experiences of students from around the world—and it didn't hurt that the international tennis players were hot!

Kristina was excited, and brought her A game. She had a vision for the program and cared about every detail. She researched each guest's homeland, paying close attention to relevant news stories coming from their region. Her goal was to discuss their country's current issues and better understand a culturally different point of view.

One particular week, Kristina planned to interview a male student from Hong Kong. In preparation, she and a friend pulled out an atlas to see where it was located on the map. It took a while to find it (hey, it's a much smaller place than a 19-year-old from Wisconsin might think). Next, they extensively researched Time magazines, newspaper headlines, and encyclopedias (no smartphones here). It was a long and exhaustive process.

By the time her Hong Kong guest arrived on set, Kristina's research was complete. As she asked him a series of questions, Kristina received only nods as responses. She persevered, peppering him with inquiries, yet her guest uttered not a single word. As it turned out, the producer, whose job was to book the guests, hadn't learned that her guest did not speak English. After this disastrous episode, Kristina realized she couldn't leave it up to others to fulfill her vision, so she "fired" the producer and began producing her own shows.

Kristina's other guest interactions were more successful, and, over time, her interview style improved. She loved the experience and wanted to pursue broadcast journalism after college. Having interviewed 12 students, she had secured hours of footage. Her next step? Create a resume reel.

In addition to "International Insights," Kristina also worked at the NBC affiliate in Green Bay, four hours away. Her job as a camerawoman and teleprompter operator gave her access to the entire news team and the studio during off hours. To supplement her interview recordings, Kristina asked colleagues to shoot footage of her reading feature stories at the news desk. She knew she should capitalize on her television hosting experience and create a resume reel.

She showed the reel to Joe, a sportscaster friend at a different station. As Joe pressed play on the VCR, Kristina's excitement veered into nerves. She had not realized until they started watching the video together how anxious she was to receive his approval and encouragement. As the video began, Joe uttered, "Hmm. Okay. Oh. Okay.

Hmmmm. Ummm. That's good—when you make expressions using your eyebrows. Uh-huh. Oh. Okay."

Kristina sat frozen. Each word felt like a stab to her confidence. With such little experience and no context, Joe's feedback felt disheartening. She didn't know how to ask for what she needed: support, guidance, a cheerleader, and a plan. And because she received a tepid response, she ended up putting the resume tape away, and instead went into advertising.

::

Despite her interest in broadcast journalism, Kristina unintentionally let this situation determine her professional path. If she had known to seek out a mentor, she could have asked the executive producer for help. Had she cultivated a community who could guide and support her, she might have been the next Hoda Kotb.

Kristina was clear about her intention to be a broadcast journalist. She had developed good habits over the years—including asking for feedback—but she didn't know what to ask nor from whom. Bottom line: *she didn't know what she didn't know.*

You, on the other hand, are better poised to share your voice and achieve your career goals. Personal and professional development is a "thing" now. Mentors are a part of our regular business lexicon. Through the process of reading and carrying out the exercises in this book, you have placed yourself solidly on the path to developing a courageous mindset, creating persuasive content, and learning the physical behaviors you will need to craft the impression you want to create. That's the good news.

The less good news is it takes great effort to reinforce positive habits and change the behaviors that are not serving you.

Behavior Change Is Hard

Behavior change is not "one and done." And the more determined we are, the more we want to see results—now! A desire to see immediate results is pervasive among ambitious people, and in the corporate world.

::

A few years ago, I worked with a San Francisco-based company whose cultural problems made news headlines. They hired me because they wanted to improve their toxic team relationships with a workshop focused on feedback. During our initial conversation, we discussed how the process of creating a feedback culture requires dedication, practice, and accountability. I proposed a multi-part plan for implementing the culture change they desired. In the end, they would commit to only one two-hour workshop focused on feedback. What are the odds that this team improved their culture and team dynamics with just a single two-hour workshop? I think you get the idea. Pretty close to zero.

::

Habits are created by repeating behaviors over years, and even decades. The results often appear incrementally, which is anathema to our drive-through, convenience-focused culture. Think about examples of behavior change in your life:

- You switch jobs and continue to get off at the subway stop near your old office
- You move to a new zip code and type in your old one when the gas pump prompts you for it
- You refer to the prior year when writing the date well into the new year

How Behaviors Are Created

Psychologists use the Hierarchy of Competence to explain how new behaviors are created. The four-level approach starts with *unconscious incompetence*. At this level, you are like Kristina; you don't know what you don't know.

At the next level, you become *consciously incompetent*. In other words, you are *aware* of what you don't know. When Kristina finally asked a mentor for feedback, she learned she spoke too quietly. She was now conscious of the problem, even if she didn't know what to do with that information.

In future interviews, Kristina intentionally projected her voice. This requires effort and represents *conscious competence*. Over years of practice, Kristina became *unconsciously competent*. She now projects her voice without thinking about it.

Before you read this book you, too, were unconsciously incompetent about aspects of speaking up. For example, you may have been unaware how often you used filler words.

You moved to conscious incompetence once you completed your vocal assessment in Chapter 4, and realized you need to remove the word "like" and the filler "um" from your communication.

In reading the Voice chapter and practicing the sticky note exercise, you worked toward conscious competence. Now you are getting in the habit of pausing after each "digestible chunk," and intentionally pause when you speak to your family and friends. With dedication, practice, and accountability, you will become unconsciously competent and naturally incorporate pauses instead of fillers whenever you speak.

How to Create New Habits

Research shows that when people intentionally focus on and practice one behavior every day consistently for 21 days, that behavior becomes a habit. That may *sound* easy, but remembering to practice for three whole weeks can be challenging. Anyone who has vowed to meditate daily or give up sugar knows this to be true.

So how can you create behavior change? You can create behavior change through these three strategies:

1. Reinforce your intention

Look back at your Speak Up goals in the Introduction to remind yourself why you want to share your voice. When you focus on why you want to communicate, you prime yourself to look for situations that reinforce your intention. This is a form of the Baader-Meinhof phenomenon, where something you've recently learned (or focused on) suddenly appears everywhere.

Exercise 1 provides an opportunity to revisit and reaffirm your goals.

2. Create realistic expectations

To meet your goals, set realistic expectations. We often try to "boil the ocean," but research—and anecdotal evidence—confirms that behavior change works best when you focus on no more than three areas to improve at a time.

I know what you're thinking. *"She said to identify three areas, but if I focus on four or five, I'll become a better communicator much faster!"*

Au contraire, mon frère. Pack away your overachieving tendencies and create small, achievable goals, also known as micro-goals.

Here is my personal experience with focusing on too many behavior changes at once. When I met my husband, a golfer, I decided I should take up the sport. We went to a driving range where I felt pretty good hitting balls. I actually made contact with (most of) the balls and many of them traveled pretty far. Success! I decided to sign up for a golf lesson.

When I met the instructor, he rattled off a list of instructions:

- Plant your feet hip-distance apart, knees bent
- Bend at the waist, but not too far
- You
- Get
- The
- Picture

With the long list of instructions now bouncing in my brain, I could no longer make contact with a single ball. *Not one!* Before the lesson I was enjoying a new sport, despite my poor techniques. But during the lesson, I became so overwhelmed and frustrated that I waited over 15 years to take my second.

The point of this story is: we simply cannot focus on too many behaviors at once. If we do, we accomplish nothing.

Create micro-goals instead, which are proven to work better than large, often unachievable goals. New Year's Resolutions, post-Covid declarations, and big sweeping plans are likely to fail without micro-goals.

We can so easily set ourselves up for failure if we vow to wake up every day at 5 am to run five miles, or to attend a hot yoga class.

Instead, schedule a 20-minute run every other day, or hot yoga 3x/week.

The same ideology applies to speaking goals.

3. Create a plan

The Power of Habit identifies three steps to creating a new habit: a cue, a routine, and a reward. To apply this model to speaking up, let's use the habit, "analyze your audience before you present."

First, identify a simple cue. This could be to set an alarm 30 minutes before your meetings to give yourself time to assess your audience.

Next, create a routine: when your alarm goes off, analyze your audience using the list of questions in Chapter 7.

Lastly, reward your routine. This can be something simple like tracking your success in a notebook or creating a "star list" where you place stickers on a calendar to indicate how many times you accomplished the task. There's a reason why we use stickers as rewards for children—they see it as a visual accolade, and, well, whaddayaknow? Adults do, too. You can also reward yourself with a treat like a flavored latte each time you finish your routine.

To establish new vocal habits, Voice Diva D'Arcy suggests, "Practice and focus for six months to a year to create those new neural pathways, and then it will begin to, as I like to say, 'seep into your bones.' Then you don't have to think about it."

Accountability

Micro-goals and the three components of creating habits seem straightforward. However, we typically make commitments when we feel strong and resourceful. When life intrudes and we feel tired, depleted, or low on resources, it's very difficult to keep our promise, even to ourselves. This is where accountability comes in. Three effective ways to create accountability include leveraging a:

1. Community

We are all influenced by our community, and it shows up in a number of ways. Influence can be bad (hello, groupthink), not great (a room full of yogis who begin to wobble when the teacher falls out of tree pose), or positive (your team competing to see who earns the most daily steps).

Research shows that relying on a community can promote behavior change, as evidenced by groups like Alcoholics Anonymous or Weight Watchers. Positive thinking within a collective can be the best kind of contagious.

::

Community has played a transformative role in my work life and in writing this book. Five years ago, I joined Tara Mohr's Playing Big course for women "who want to play bigger in their work and their lives." During the 12-week virtual course we explored a topic that correlated to a chapter in the Playing Big book, ranging from "Discovering your Inner Mentor" to "Quieting the Inner Critic" and "Unhooking from Praise and Criticism."

When the 12-week program was complete, she encouraged participants to create a "Small Group," which is an accountability system to keep participants in the process. I connected with six women interested in meeting biweekly to hold rich, important discussions, ending with a call to action.

::

Today, we serve as mentors, supports, and accountability partners for each other. For four years, we have been meeting together, and in that time, we have designed and executed career "leaps," started and grown businesses, and re-aligned our careers to our North Stars. As one of our Small Group members recently said, "I understand more deeply, the importance of camaraderie in finding support, accountability, and encouragement."

Identify an existing community.

Okay. You may be sold on the idea of a community, but now what? Where do you find one? Depending on what aspect of speaking up is most important to you, I guarantee there is an established community for you.

- Toastmasters is a program that creates opportunities to "practice public speaking, improve your communication, and build leadership skills." Community groups are located throughout the world, and corporate groups exist at many companies.
- Improv classes are a great way to think on your feet and practice speaking in front of others.
- Tara Mohr's Playing Big course is an excellent life and career coaching group.
- Facebook has a plethora (as in the ultimate motherlode) of specialty groups you can join.
- Many communities have co-working spaces with built-in communities. In the San Francisco Bay Area, The Hivery is a "co-working space and inspiration lab."

Create your own community

Just as you have book clubs, movie clubs and cooking clubs, you can create a Speak Up club. Like your other clubs, community-based groups need structure, and at least one champion, to succeed. Best practices for forming your own community-based club include:

- Establish (realistic) expectations about meeting frequency, attendance expectations, and roles for the host and participants. (In my experience, punitive threats are less effective than providing support and rewards for attending.)
- Alternate hosting duties.
- Communicate the guidelines clearly and regularly.

Dive In!

Whether you join a community or create one on your own, taking a proactive role will yield better results. It's not always easy to talk at networking events and the like, but the initiative pays off. Here is my experience with this:

::

Last September I attended a networking event where I didn't know a soul. I wanted to look good, so I donned a hip, coated moto jacket (a bad idea on this particular fall day) then headed into an industrial-chic former warehouse to meet my 100 new . . . Best friends? Competitors? Acquaintances? The common thread among us was a passion for keynote speaking, yet our years of experience, our success, and our pathways were wildly different. There was opportunity there. And there was fear. My body responded with damp armpits and a dry mouth.

As I walked into the crowd of people, I initiated Conversation #1, which was awwwwkward. I nailed my elevator pitch, but guess what? At 8:50 am in a very crowded space, launching into a 30-second rehearsed speech felt corny, trite, inappropriate. So, I opted for the language of networking events: small talk.

"Where are you in from?" I asked.

"Chicago," he replied.

Being the smooth conversationalist I am, I followed up with, "Are you in the city or in a suburb?" This led to a dead end. Other than at the airport, I've never been to Chicago!

Conversation #2 held more promise. He was from my geographic area! He was on a similar career path! He enrolled in a certification program I completed a few years ago! We had kids the same age! Synergy potential bloomed. Then, it withered as the crowd surged, conversations splintered, and there was no further conversation with this potential connection.

Copy and paste these conversations throughout the morning. God, this networking process can be exhausting—even for an extrovert.

By lunchtime, the room appeared to relax. Rather than a herd of people standing in tight circles, people were spread out, relaxing on couches. Conversations were happening at a slower pace. There was more discussion and less interrogation. During the remainder of the day, I met a half-dozen people whose life and career experiences we shared in detail. We found connections as we shared successes and failures.

::

Now that the networking event is over, these are the people I go to when I have a question or need support. The opportunity for community is out there. It can feel hard to initiate and navigate, but magic happens once you dive in and swim.

2. Accountability partner

In addition to (or in place of) a community, an accountability partner can help you stay in the communication improvement process. With a single partner, you can go deeper and receive or provide more customized support.

Having a partner is also helpful because they create perspective when we can't see it ourselves. (Remember our biases from Chapter 6?) They also provide a mirror, demonstrating opportunities for us to advocate for ourselves. I know I need this level of support.

::

In my coaching work, I have a cancellation policy that I communicate to clients. Inevitably, life happens, and people occasionally need to cancel an appointment. I typically give clients a one-time pass, then reiterate the policy. When a client cancels again at the last moment, I find it very hard to enforce my own policy, yet I always advise friends and colleagues to enforce theirs.

::

It's invaluable to have a buddy who reminds you of your goals, your purpose for speaking up, and who supports you when you falter. One of my clients, Tia, hired me as her accountability coach. She is a diligent worker who practices her projection every week, but she wanted the additional support of a coach who reviewed her recorded rehearsals. After six months of consistent practice, she has been promoted.

While hiring a coach is a luxury, with a plan, regular practice, and accountability, you can make significant progress—no coach required! In fact, you can leverage multiple types of support. You can cultivate a community for one purpose (say, improv practice) and an accountability partner for another purpose (like building your confidence through your mindset). I take part in my *Playing Big* group as a way to remain inspired, to help me make leaps and grow my business. Meanwhile, I carve out time for an accountability partner who will help me stay on task and meet writing deadlines.

Tool or App

Another option for creating accountability is using online tools or apps. There are many accountability apps available that guide you through goal setting and tracking and are tied to financial incentives or punishments.

Other apps are designed for specific areas of speaking up including:

- Increasing your awareness and reducing your use of filler words.
- Helping with stage fright.

The Resource section at the end of this book lists tools to help you with accountability and all aspects of speaking up.

If I can leave you with one piece of advice about accountability, it's "practice makes progress" and, "aim for progress, not perfection." Ok, that's two pieces of advice. But note, I'm not sharing five or six pieces of advice.

"We don't have to do all of it alone. We were never meant to."

BRENÉ BROWN

EXERCISES

Exercise 1: Select Areas to Improve

What: Identify up to three behaviors to better develop your communication.

Why: To improve your Speak Up skills, it's important to make a plan.

How: Start your plan by writing in your Speak Up journal about the skills you'd like to improve

1. Pick one item to improve from the pivotal physical delivery list of Pause, Connect & Energy:
   - Include pauses (or breaths) between statements
   - Hold eye contact long enough to connect with each person in the room
   - Display warmth when you communicate
   - Use different expressions to animate your content (e.g., raising eyebrows)
   - Utilize vocal modulation to create passion and interest

   The behavior I plan to improve (Speak Up Skill #1) is:

2. Choose one or two behaviors from the list below:
   - Vary your volume or speed as you talk
   - Emphasize specific words and phrases
   - Use natural and welcoming body language
   - Use symmetrical body language
   - Determine and adapt to your listeners' needs and motivations
   - State the Bottom Line On Top
   - Structure your content in three parts
   - Include benefits or relevance to your listener
   - Flip your script and repeat it like a mantra
   - Positive self-talk while you communicate
   - Identify and practice a cognitive, physical, or audience-focused nerve strategy
   - Rehearse before everyday meetings

Write your selections in your Speak Up journal.

Speak Up Skill #2:

Speak Up Skill #3:

Exercise 2: Create a Plan

What: Get clear about how you will create new Speak Up habits.

Why: When you create a detailed plan, you are more likely to follow through.

How: Answer the following questions in your journal. An example of answers is listed in parentheses:

What will you do to improve Speak Up Skill #1? (Review videos to see if my facial expressions were warm during my meetings)

What will you do to improve Speak Up Skill #2? (Write the bottom line before I attend each meeting)

What will you do to improve Speak Up Skill #3? (State my flipped script whenever I enter a meeting with people who intimidate me)

When will you practice? (First thing in the morning before others arrive)

Where will you practice? (At my desk)

How long will you dedicate to practicing? (10 minutes a day)

Can you create a fun term or word for your practice? (CEO Prep)

How will you remember to practice? (Set a calendar reminder)

How will you hold yourself accountable? (Accountability partner and a monthly check-in with my manager to see if she thinks I have improved)

Who will be your accountability partner? (My colleague who is focusing on her meeting presence)

Identify specific benchmarks to help you stay focused and accountable. (Monthly manager professional check-ins)

How will you celebrate sticking to these benchmarks? (Take a bath with a delicious glass of wine)

How will you overcome obstacles that arise? (Block 30 minutes in my calendar each day to make sure I focus on my Speak Up Skills)

Exercise 3: Visualize Success

What: A journaling activity to visualize your Speak Up Success.

Why: Visualization is correlated with behavioral success.

How: Answer the following questions in your journal.

1. How will improving your Speak Up Skills help your:
   - Confidence
   - Career
   - Relationship with others
   - Reputation at work
   - Other areas in your life
2. Where do you see yourself in five years? Get as specific as possible. How does speaking up help you achieve your goals?
3. Write down a list of people who support you. Consider reaching out and asking for support or simply know that these people are on your team; perceived support is correlated with goal attainment.

Closing

Three years ago, I entered a board room and was greeted by Mike, a sandy-haired tech CEO in his 50s. Dressed in khakis and a button-down shirt, he welcomed me with a full smile, eyes that sparkled, and a bear-paw handshake. He appeared amiable and lovely on the surface, yet just below that his personality was cold, hard steel. I knew this because I had been warned. I also knew because I had worked with his type many times: the seasoned executive with a no-bullshit core who is wise enough to amp up his charm at exactly the right moments.

Mike sat at the head of the table while I took the seat to his right. The room was quiet as we waited for someone to take charge and start the meeting. The seven other attendees were perched around the large room expectantly. The silence was awkward and disconcerting.

At that point in time, 12 years had elapsed since my mortifying "brown and fizzy" moment, and in the years since, I'd coached over one thousand leaders. (Side note: Typically, when I'm hired to prep an executive for a high-stakes presentation, we meet several times to build rapport, establish expectations, and begin the planning process. In this case, Mike had canceled every prep call—all three. So it was just days away from the event I was asked to help Mike present at when I met him for the first time, as he was surrounded by his team who appeared scared into submission.)

Okay, but let's get back to the story.

Mike's chief of staff broke the silence by establishing some context. "As we know, the event is in four days. Since other obligations prevented us from preparing, now is the time to focus." Then Mike took the reins and started talking about investment philosophies, and the history of banking. The room remained stone-faced. I was confused. The philosophy of investing? The evolution of banking? Mike was scheduled to speak to entrepreneurs about how to raise funds for their start-ups. History and philosophy would not resonate.

I looked around the room waiting for a member of his team to speak up. Nothing. Mike droned on. "The Pittsburgh steel magnates created success by . . . "

We had been sitting in the room for 14 minutes, and no one had spoken more than two sentences except Mike, who was waxing on about real estate titans. I was hesitant to interrupt him, and he did not appear open to feedback or new ideas. While I hadn't yet had any opportunities to earn credibility with Mike or his team, I couldn't sit silently listening to a history lesson when I was tasked to prepare him for an audience of over 200 entrepreneurs.

Ugh. I felt nauseous.

When I glanced around the room to observe Mike's team's faces, they appeared to be holding their breath. I felt the bile rising up to my throat, the heat to my cheeks. The feeling reminded me of standing on the edge of a cliff looking down—way down—at the sparkling water below. But I wasn't ready to jump.

I reminded myself, "I know how to work with Mike. I've worked with people like him dozens of times before." I thought about the bigger picture: "Mike is a regular person. If he hates what I have to say, so be it. I have other clients who value my work."

After taking a deep breath, I dove in. "Excuse me, Mike. Before we proceed, let's take a step back. It's important to think about the audience. We need to identify what they want to hear, and the value they will gain from your talk. Let's start there."

Speaking up takes courage (and, for me, twelve years of practice). The "brown and fizzy" me would have apologized ("I'm sorry, Mike"), or asked for permission ("Would it be okay to . . . "), or equivocated

("Maybe could we consider . . . "). Or perhaps I would not have said anything at all.

But I did speak up, and the energy in the room shifted. I felt the room collectively exhale. Mike, on the other hand, looked stunned. "Has no one interrupted him before?" I wondered. He recovered quickly, processed the idea, and nodded his approval. With that, I hopped up from the table, grabbed a few Sharpies, and printed "Audience Analysis" on the top of the whiteboard.

We spent the next chunk of time dissecting the audience, identifying objectives, and composing three clear, crisp messages. Next, we outlined his talk with a more compelling and audience-friendly framework.

After two hours of systematic prep, the culmination of our work was scribbled across the expanse of the whiteboard. "Okay," I said. "You're ready." All six heads swiveled away from the whiteboard and stared . . . at me. Rather than admit he was not, Mike stammered, "Well, sure, we've made interesting progress. As soon as I rewrite the script, I'll be ready."

I interjected again. "Let's try something," I gently countered. "Look at the outline we created. Speak through it to determine if it meets the objectives." Mike tentatively agreed and "presented" his outline. The transitions were rocky, but he'd mostly delivered a cohesive presentation.

"Okay, how did that feel?" I asked. The teddy bear I first met at the start of the meeting returned, and his face broke into a wide smile. "It felt great! Did it sound as good as it felt?" He looked around the room for his team to validate. While I suspected they agreed with most, if not all, statements that generally emerged from Mike's mouth, it was their enthusiastic nods and exuberant gushing that confirmed we had made true progress.

::

True progress. Try to think about what that looks and feels like for you. I once felt a deep sense of embarrassment for asking a simple question. Now I take great pride in having made it my profession. By following the lessons and exercises contained in this book, I now:

- Take initiative
- Push through vulnerability
- Share relevant content
- Engage my listeners
- Speak passionately
- Appear confident
- Share my voice at work

And my 2,000 clients do, too. Let's review by taking a quick peek at where some of them are now.

Gabriela (Chapter 1) has mastered the pause, and continues to move up the corporate ladder. If you were to ask newer employees of PetBest (as I have), they would tell you how shocked they are to learn she was once viewed as lacking gravitas.

Keisha (Chapter 2) has been promoted several times over and is now responsible for the training of all new employees. She continues to prioritize connection.

Kristina (Chapters 6 and 14) secured a mentor—many of them, in fact—and in the 10 years since hiding her resume reel, she's written a book, leads corporate workshops, and shares her voice regularly. And boldly!

Zahara (Chapter 12) has become more genuine. Her sustainability idea was eventually implemented. She still struggles with perfectionism, but she's working on it. Progress, not rigid precision.

Jessy (Chapter 11) is killing it! She has become a regular at board meetings, she mentors and inspires the young women in her company, and she placed a large sign in her office that says, "The challenging and scary moments become my proudest accomplishments." Yes, motivational signs can be cheesy and induce dumb chills, but not when Jessy rocks her authenticity and confidence.

Bronwyn, meanwhile, (Chapter 6) is high-kicking her way across social media—and, let's be honest, the world—with her podcast entitled *20 Minutes with Bronwyn*. She has thousands of followers and is an in-demand speaker.

The only casualty in this story is Marq. Remember the Shakespeare-loving leader in Chapter 7? He did not heed my advice and, sadly, he was fired. But are you surprised? The silver lining is he has a lot more time on his hands to recite Shakespeare . . . to himself.

The other "characters" in this book, and the 1,967 additional clients I have worked with, see real improvement when they:

- Practice at least once a week,
- Commit to improving their communication skills for three or more months, and
- Create an accountability plan.

When they meet these conditions, they improve. *Every single one of them.*

Across the United States, women's business standings have also improved, albeit slowly. Between 2015 and 2020, 5% more women held senior vice president roles (from 23% to 28%) and there were 4% more women in C-suite positions (from 17% to 21%). Of course, the pandemic reversed some of this important progress. The optimist in me notes that the pandemic also allowed people to bring more of themselves to work. Babies on laps, toddlers asking for snacks, and roommates in the background of work meetings are no longer taboo. Hybrid working has the potential to provide opportunities for women to speak up, even from their living room.

Regardless of where you sit (literally or metaphorically), what the world needs is to hear your voice, your perspective, and your ideas. The demographics of the United States are becoming more diverse and more interesting. The people who ascend to leadership roles, and the ideas that are implemented throughout, should reflect the richness we see in our cities and across our country.

So, what now? Well, you have read this book, completed the exercises, and made a plan for yourself. And the best part is you're continuing to improve. Now, dear reader, it is time to share your voice. Trust me on this. The world needs **you**.

"Tell me, what is it you plan to do with your one wild and precious life?"

MARY OLIVER

SPEAK UP TENETS

- How your body feels when you speak is always different than what you see or hear upon playback of the recording.
- Pause, Connection, and Energy are a magical trifecta.
- People rehearse for important events but rarely for day-to-day meetings and interactions. Start rehearing your regular updates!
- Rapid speakers think the answer is to slow down. Instead, keep an animated pace and pause to let your listeners absorb your ideas.
- Even if you think you're adapting to your audience's needs—their values and their communication style—you're likely not adapting enough.
- Don't worry too much about body language.
- An animated presentation is always more engaging and memorable than an accurate presentation.
- We think our mistakes are a big deal, but our listeners tend not to notice. And when they do, they quickly forget.
- Communicating as if you are part of a conversation is always better than presenting.
- Strength and warmth are key to being a good communicator (and leader, too!).
- Structure is the communication scaffolding your audience needs.

Resources

There are hundreds of resources in the world that complement *Speak Up, Dammit!* Here are a few of my favorites.

Cabane, Olivia Fox. *The Charisma Myth: How Anyone Can Master the Art and Science of Personal Magnetism*. New York: Portfolio, 2012.

Cain, Susan. *Quiet: The Power of Introverts in a World That Can't Stop Talking*. New York: Crown Publishing, 2013.

Clark, Dorie. *Stand Out: How to Find Your Breakthrough Idea and Build a Following Around It*. New York: Portfolio, 2015.

Duarte, Nancy. *Slide:ology: The Art and Science of Creating Great Presentations*. Sebastopol, CA: O'Reilly Media, 2008.

Duhigg, Charles. *The Power of Habit: Why We Do What We Do in Life and Business*. New York: Random House, 2012.

Helgesen, Sally and Goldsmith, Marshall. *How Women Rise: Break the 12 Habits Holding You Back from Your Next Raise, Promotion, or Job*. New York: Hachette Books, 2018.

Ibarra, Herminia. *Act Like a Leader, Think Like a Leader*. Boston: Harvard Business Review Press, 2015.

Mohr, Tara. *Playing Big: Find Your Voice, Your Mission, Your Message*. Penguin Publishing, 2014.

Simpson, Kate and Ellen Watson. *Take Two: A Journal for New Beginnings*. San Francisco: Chronicle Books, 2020

Podcasts

Abrahams, Matt. *Think Fast, Talk Smart.* https://www.gsb.stanford.edu/insights/think-fast-talk-smart-podcast

Beyer, Johanna and Morrow, Kim. *Inside Journey.* https://www.insidejourney.com/

Harts, Minda. #SecureTheSeat. https://www.mindaharts.com/podcast

Saglimbeni, Bronwyn. *20 Minutes with Bronwyn.* https://www.bronwyncommunications.com/podcast

Apps and Tools

Astound: Voice & Speech Coach

LikeSo: Speech recording improvement

Otter: Transcribe Voice Notes

Voice Memos on iPhone

TED Talks / YouTube Videos

TED Talk: "Your Body Language May Shape Who You Are" by Amy Cuddy. https://www.ted.com/talks/amy_cuddy_your_body_language_may_shape_who_you_are/up-next?language=en

YouTube: "Problematizing Persuasion" by Shawon Jackson at Stanford Business School. https://www.youtube.com/watch?v=KiDICCxS06Y

Websites

The Hivery Community, Coworking, and Inspiration Lab: https://www.thehivery.com/

The Playing Big Journey: https://playingbig.org/home/

The Work of Byron Katie: https://thework.com/

Acknowledgements

Although there is only one name on the cover, *Speak Up, Dammit!* would not exist if it weren't for a band of steady supporters who contributed along the way.

To my A-Team: Kristina Paider, Ellen Watson, Jane Wilson, Allegra Bandy, and Emily Evans, you tirelessly inspired, coached, coaxed, edited, and pushed this baby forward. Thank you!

My heartfelt appreciation goes to:

The dozens of women I interviewed. Your stories are important, and I hope you enjoyed reliving them here.

The advanced readers who asked questions, thereby altering the book for the better.

The authors who supported me along the way. You are a special and generous group.

The behind-the-scenes crew—Carla, Lara, Dave, Michelle, and dedicated Carlyn. For you, I am grateful!

My family, friends, and a global list of supporters. You listened, advised, and cheered me on throughout, and I appreciate each one of you!

Most of all, I thank the many, many people who have trusted me in a coaching or training environment. By sharing your struggles with me and allowing us to experiment, you—and I—have grown as a result. I am inspired by your bravery and your pursuit of improvement. Our experiences together are the inspiration for this book.

About the Author

Hope Timberlake is a speaker, trainer and author who focuses on the communication side of leadership. She is passionate about persuasive messaging, executive presence, and elevating the voices of women and those underrepresented in leadership.

Hope works with executives and their teams at leading companies including AirBnB, Autodesk, BlackRock, Dropbox, Intel, PlayStation, Splunk, and many scaling start-ups.

By creating rapport and building trust, Hope empowers people to excel as communicators and leaders. Her energy and creativity make her keynotes and workshops impactful and engaging. She is particularly proud of her Speak Up Masterclass series. The multi-week virtual courses are filled with exercises and individual feedback that leave participants feeling confident and inspired.

Hope earned her Bachelor of Arts degree from Duke University and completed a Masters degree at University of California, Berkeley. She lives in the San Francisco Bay Area with her husband, teenaged children and dog Mona.

To find out more information about Hope and the Speak Up Masterclass series, please visit www.hopetimberlake.com